Not Proud

A Smorgasbord of Shame

Edited by Scott Huot and GW Brazier

SSE

SIMON SPOTLIGHT ENTERTAINMENT
New York London Toronto Sydney

To Eileen McEvoy

SSE

SIMON SPOTLIGHT ENTERTAINMENT
An imprint of Simon & Schuster
1230 Avenue of the Americas, New York, New York 10020
Text copyright © 2003, 2005 by Scott Huot & GW Brazier
All rights reserved, including the right of reproduction in whole or in part in any form.
SIMON SPOTLIGHT ENTERTAINMENT and related logo are trademarks of Simon & Schuster, Inc.
Manufactured in Mexico
First Edition 10 9 8 7 6 5 4 3 2 1
Library of Congress Cataloging-in-Publication Data
Not proud : a smorgasbord of shame / [selected] by Scott Huot and GW Brazier.— 1st ed.
p. cm.
Confessions anonymously contributed to www.notproud.com.
Includes bibliographical references and index.
ISBN 0-689-87797-8 (alk. paper)
1. Wit and humor. I. Huot, Scott. II. Brazier, G. W.
PN6153.N68 2005
818'.60208—dc22
2004019775

This is a revised and expanded version of the book *Murder, Incest and Cat Food Sandwiches*, published in Canada by Rank Products.

Contents

One night more than four years ago, we made a box that we hoped the world would fill.

We called this box Notproud.com and we hoped to fill it with sins, transgressions, and regrets. A quarter of a million words later, the box is no longer empty, and we have borne witness to the best and worst of human behavior.

This book is the result of reading and weighing more than twenty thousand anonymous confessions from across the globe. The religious, the spiritual, the pragmatic, and the irreverent have all dropped by, donating moments of their lives to this testament you hold in your hands.

Along the way we have learned a few things about ourselves and the world around us:

1) Human curiosity feeds the voyeur within.

Peering in on the trials and tribulations of others is an intriguing, unsettling, and, at times, a very comforting activity. It's why we slow down to look at car wrecks, why tabloid talk shows thrive, and why reality television has tantalized the world's cultural palette. They allow us to see that where we are could have been much worse.

2) We're not just passive onlookers; we're also active participants.

The need to mark one's place in the world is instinctual. We have an innate desire to be heard and understood. The anonymity of an online confessional allows us to be as candid as we want without the fear of consequence or judgment. It allows us to share the secrets that trouble our souls in a way that day-to-day living does not often provide.

3) We are not alone.
You may find yourself in this collection, either through your own words, or through the feeling that someone somewhere else has traveled down the very same path. These confessions shine a spotlight into the many dim corners of our collective psyches. So, sit back, turn the page, and prepare to meet your neighbors.

Scott Huot & GW Brazier
Founders of Notproud.com

All confessions are anonymous. There are those that may contain ideas or words offensive to some. Confessions reflect how we see ourselves. It is not always pretty, but it is often illuminating.

Pride

02/17/2004 at 22:32:46
I sometimes belittle other people in order to feel a flashing
moment of intellectual superiority. In truth, I'm terrified.
Of everything.

Not Proud

10/29/2003 at 19:47:24
They say that the world would be a boring place if everyone were the exact same. Yet when I think of how interesting I am and what a pleasure I am to be around, I can't help but realize that a world full of me's would be absolutely brilliant.

03/15/2001 at 00:57:19
I'm a borderline genius and I have a really hot body. It makes
people nervous.

Not Proud

01/20/2002 at 07:57:59
I'm not bad looking, but for years I have deliberately cut myself
and scarred my body so people like me for my personality, and
not my appearance.

12/18/2000 at 01:30:53
I can only be friends with girls who are uglier than me. I hate
competition.

Not Proud

10/12/2000 at 17:29:05
I take pride in pointing out the shortcomings of others and making them feel bad about it.

10/08/2003 at 18:36:00
I left my wife. She was not a "suitable" person to "grow" with.
Now I am a junkie and unsuitable to walk into a restaurant.

Not Proud

02/28/2004 at 03:11:35
I kick ass on the bass guitar. People see it too, and then they
think it's weird that I'm kind of conceited. But they aren't the
ones kicking so much ass.

12/15/2001 at 00:04:10

I am ashamed of my job. It's not illegal or even dirty; I just feel it is beneath me. It is moron's work, idiot labor. I should be thinking and creating and excelling, not lugging boxes and pounding keyboards. I am slowly atrophying.

Not Proud

04/02/2001 at 15:19:07
I am too proud to talk to my therapist. As stupid as it sounds, I don't want her to think that I'm f*cked up. . . . I care what she thinks of me. Why the hell am I paying eighty dollars a session then? I want someone to care, but I don't want them to think I'm weak. . . . God, how pathetic.

04/01/2002 at 03:17:58
My pride as a doctor led me to misdiagnose a patient, who then went blind as a result.

Not Proud

11/01/2000 at 15:57:52
If I walk up to a urinal to take a leak and there's a guy at the urinal next to me, I'll make sure to pee into a hole in the bottom of the urinal so my pee sounds louder and it seems like I have a bigger cock. That's just what I do.

12/16/2003 at 01:18:51
I have a serious drug problem. I have too much pride to ask for help. Pride is harder to overcome than the drugs themselves.

Not Proud

09/15/2000 at 12:38:57

I was having dinner at my parents' house the other day and I just snapped. I destroyed my high school graduation photo. It's been the cause of far too many embarrassing situations. My mom was really hurt, my dad was pissed, and I cut my hand on the glass, but man was it worth it. I couldn't stand to see that naturally feathered hair, parted down the middle, any damn longer.

02/26/2001 at 14:09:08
Pride has forced me to ignore my husband's infidelities 'cause
I just can't handle people knowing how he treats me.

Not Proud

11/23/2000 at 13:29:49
I can't even leave the house to buy a carton of milk without getting all teased and made-up. Then I spend close to an hour each night removing all the crap. I hate the routine, but you never know who might be looking.

09/02/2001 at 03:14:58
I'm proud that I'm a lot better looking than my best friend.
Then again, a lot of people are.

Not Proud

11/20/2002 at 05:27:01

I own the coolest record store in town and I can make people listen to really bad music whenever I'm grumpy. Sometimes I do the baddest farts you've ever smelled, especially when there are annoying customers around.

03/09/2004 at 17:01:15
Although I have a loving boyfriend, I keep flirting with anyone
I find attractive, including his friends. I have no self-esteem. I
can't stand criticism. I am what others think of me. The more
people think I'm great, the better I feel.

Not Proud

12/05/2001 at 20:23:46
I can drink everybody I know under the table. I used to feel good about this . . . but now I'm not so sure.

05/02/2001 at 10:24:29
I am proud that I am a twenty-one-year-old woman who knows
how to change a flat tire by herself. That really comes in handy
when you have a piece of shit car.

Not Proud

09/04/2002 at 14:58:45
I am proud of my naturally blond hair and beautiful feet. I am also proud that I have been quite the libertine but everyone suspects me of being a virgin. I am a stealth slut.

07/02/2002 at 21:36:51
I am not proud of the fact that I write music for pornos.

Not Proud

12/29/2001 at 07:18:09
I have worn foundation every single day since I turned thirteen.
I am almost twenty-four now. I can't stand for anyone to look
at my naked skin.

07/06/2002 at 01:50:36
I love to set fire to homes, buildings, cars, etc. I once set fire to a housing development in its construction phase. I'm talking about millions of dollars lost, up in smoke. It was great seeing the fire trucks and police all around. I set fire to a car that was in a parking garage. It's great how fire just grows exponentially from a match light to a raging monster. More to come.

Not Proud

12/29/2001 at 03:02:27
For all my failures, I still have not molested a child or raped a woman, attacked a coworker, embezzled, taken drugs, or kicked anybody when they were down. I work to make my home a nicer place, put food on the table, and stay with a woman I don't love for the sake of my child.

02/16/2003 at 15:46:44
When I was ten I accidentally killed the school bully in a play-
ground fight and I am kind of proud of it.

Envy

10/16/2000 at 17:11:00
I measure my accomplishments by the weaknesses and failures
of others.

Not Proud

10/12/2000 at 17:46:04
I envy all those who walk up to beautiful women . . . and walk away with them.

03/09/2004 at 21:41:04
This bothers me: People tell me that my brother is a good-looking guy, and then mention that I don't look a thing like him. There are only a few conclusions I can make, and I don't really like any of them.

Not Proud

04/03/2002 at 17:39:37
I envy people who have companionship. Most of the time I drink alone.

02/10/2002 at 23:04:46
Forgive me for not attending your wedding, but I couldn't bear
to see you walk down the aisle when I still feel the way I do
about you.

Not Proud

12/29/2001 at 00:33:43
I had a nice girl back in '92. I fucked around on her with everyone I could. An ex-friend married her, and she now works for NASA and lives on the beach in Florida making a bundle. Talk about fucking up.

10/08/2002 at 03:45:13
My best friend is so pretty and rich. She gets all the guys and
clothes and things she wants whenever she wants them. Her
beauty is fake, though, and only I know that. She has an eating
disorder.

Not Proud

03/26/2004 at 21:15:22
I was so envious the other day that I lied about having a Swiss bank account with millions of dollars.

10/28/2003 at 14:10:13
I am envious of everyone out there who found love in another
human being and life in general, when I could only find love in
drugs and alcohol.

Not Proud

10/05/2000 at 00:53:59
If I see a nice-looking girl out with a guy who is obviously her lover, a tiny voice in my head screams, "If you beat up the guy, the girl's yours." I blame the brain stem. I think it's got old-fashioned ideas.

02/14/2002 at 14:09:38

I envy my roommate. He's handsome and popular. He gets invited to parties, and has women all over him. What's worse is that he's a nice guy; he cares about people. The other day I was walking back from the shower wearing boxer shorts and nothing else. I couldn't be bothered to put the rest of my clothes back on when my dorm room is two doors away from the shower room. Some girls were blocking the way. I asked them to move so I could get by, they laughed and feigned vomiting with their friend after I walked past. That sort of thing doesn't happen to my roommate.

Not Proud

02/21/2004 at 18:19:35
I just realized the other day that I envied a crippled person because he was getting a lot of attention. How sick is that?

02/26/2004 at 09:17:00
My boyfriend keeps old photos in his wallet of friends and exes he still cares about. One day I noticed a photo of this slag he used to see fall out, and I just sat there, suggested we leave, and the photo became lost for eternity.

Not Proud

05/27/2004 at 02:47:50
I envy you because I was supposed to break your heart but you did it to me first, you bastard.

02/24/2002 at 10:40:33
Isn't it just unbearable to hear people fucking in the next room when you're just a horny little wanker? I find it so painful I don't even masturbate when I listen. But I still listen.

Not Proud

02/06/2001 at 04:36:51
I envy the innocence and ignorance of babies. One time when I was seven, I watched my eight-month-old brother sleeping quietly, and I slapped him, just so he would need me.

10/16/2000 at 17:28:08
I envy everyone that has someone.

Not Proud

03/22/2002 at 18:45:36
I'm glad my best friend is getting married, 'cause I'm tired of him always getting the best women.

10/24/2000 at 10:12:53

I am extremely envious of people who have friends. I am alone most of the time, and I see them, and wish I was standing there having trivial conversations and laughing and joking and making fun of that guy staring at us. . . .

Not Proud

03/07/2002 at 18:17:37
I hate all of my sisters. They're all prettier, and more loved.
I am the ugly embarrassment of the family.

04/14/2001 at 13:54:09
I'm jealous of the old generation that has social skills and role
models instead of TV and computer screens.

Not Proud

10/04/2000 at 16:11:22
I envy those who can drink and do drugs without negative consequences. I miss getting high.

03/08/2001 at 12:15:23

The sun will rise soon and a new day will begin, but not for me. In my life the sun never rises, only darkness falls around me. Morning turns to night, hours drift by without any change, without any light, without any hope. Tears stream down my face and I'm left to wonder what will happen next to me, my uneasiness leads to fear. I'm apprehensive of my future, I'm not sure I have one. I envy all those who have the courage to leave an abusive relationship.

Not Proud

02/04/2004 at 04:22:54
It pleases me to see happy people take a fall. I particularly like breakups and divorces.

07/25/2001 at 11:11:04

I am envious of my sister because she died and everyone loves her more now than ever, and they only pity me for having to live without her.

Not Proud

08/08/2001 at 22:51:04
I want to be a woman. I envy the sexual prowess that every woman seems capable of possessing. I'm a good-looking guy, but women are forces of nature.

02/02/2003 at 19:39:42

Today I read a list detailing the penis dimensions of two hundred–plus famous (and not-so-famous) rock stars as compiled by an infamous groupie and a few of her close groupie friends. (The list ain't that hard to find on any search engine.) Ninety-five percent of these rock stars had bigger dicks than I do. My band is nowhere near as famous as these guys' bands; my dick apparently is also lacking in stature. Disheartening to say the least . . .

Not Proud

10/31/2001 at 22:51:26
I envy all you kids who got more candy than me tonight. My neighborhood stinks.

08/06/2001 at 04:48:36
I want to be anyone but me.

Sloth

02/21/2001 at 17:33:21
Sleep is my best friend and my worst enemy.

Not Proud

09/10/2000 at 23:47:09
I drive everywhere. I hate to walk. I drive to buy a container of milk three blocks away. I don't even like driving. I just hate to walk.

11/23/2002 at 10:11:40

There are days that I should be doing my work. I'm a self-employed artist. Instead I surf the Web, or watch TV and call it "social and pop-culture research."

Not Proud

06/04/2004 at 11:54:58
It once took me fifteen minutes to decide to scratch my ass.

01/25/2002 at 12:20:40
My bags are still packed, even though I came home a week ago. Every dish in the house is dirty. It's filthy in here. I'm watching TV and surfing the Net and I'm sick and miserable, but I'm also lazy and it makes me feel bad for my boyfriend. It's his apartment.

Not Proud

11/16/2002 at 22:03:19
I used to go upstairs to the stockroom at work and build beds or chairs out of boxes or toilet paper, and then sit in my creation as long as possible while getting paid for it.

06/01/2004 at 14:28:18
Sometimes I shoplift things I could easily afford because I don't want to wait in line.

Not Proud

05/29/2002 at 23:43:12
I am heavily addicted to a pharmaceutical narcotic—Percocet.
And the days I run out I can't even get out of bed. I cry and I cry
and I mope and television commercials make me want to com-
mit suicide.

10/04/2000 at 12:43:57
Sometimes I pee into a two-liter bottle when I'm in bed and
getting up is just . . . not . . . an . . . option.

Not Proud

02/24/2002 at 11:48:11
I blow my nose on worn socks and underwear from my laundry
bag. I think so little of it I don't even realize I'm doing it.

10/31/2002 at 10:09:22

I have never worked a full day in my life. I often dream what it would be like to return home thinking, "Sheesh, I really worked my ass off." I'd say I work for about thirty minutes each day, the rest is spent surfing the Net and chatting to friends. I get paid well for doing absolutely nothing. And the strangest thing—I've been doing it for about two and a half years and no one seems to care. I'd recommend becoming a journalist.

Not Proud

10/05/2000 at 10:10:02
I like to be underneath where I can just get fucked.

04/02/2004 at 22:34:06

I'm so lazy that when I play video games I keep them on the easiest setting just because I can't be bothered enough to actually try and have a challenge. For example, in "NHL 2004" I've won the Stanley Cup twelve times.

Not Proud

12/25/2000 at 23:41:27
I was supposed to bring my fish home from college during the Xmas break, but I was so lazy that I just flushed them and told everybody they died of mysterious circumstances in transit.

10/05/2000 at 01:29:49
Most of the time I would rather just masturbate than deal with the crap of another person.

01/20/2002 at 08:10:53

A few years ago I tried committing suicide. There was a hook on my ceiling, and so I made a noose and put one end around my neck. The other was attached to this hook. I jumped off a chair and the hook came flying out of the ceiling. I was too lazy to try again. Sums up my life really.

01/22/2001 at 18:50:50

I bought a gym membership and paid twelve months ahead. I went twice. I feel like it would be fun to go and check out the girls' asses, but I can't seem to get off my own ass.

Not Proud

05/04/2001 at 18:48:05
My therapist told me a way to achieve inner peace was to finish
things I had started. Today I finished two bags of potato chips,
a chocolate cake, and a porn video that has been sitting inside
my VCR for two weeks. I feel better already.

03/13/2001 at 13:32:14
I never feel like I'm doing as much as I should be. I read all these autobiographies of rich, successful go-getters and they are always so much more driven than me. I wonder if you can fake drive like that, or if it's something you're born with.

Not Proud

12/08/2003 at 19:47:52
Sleep, go to work, pretend to work, avoid coworkers, come home, get high, watch TV, sleep. Repeat till I die.

03/08/2001 at 13:45:15

Once I slept for, like, five days straight and missed a week of class. So my mom took me to the doctor because she thought I had mono. The doctor's official diagnosis was that I'm just a lazy piece of shit.

Not Proud

10/04/2000 at 19:40:54
Some days I can't even get outta bed in the morning for my easy job. Then I remember I wouldn't enjoy staying home either.

09/12/2000 at 09:30:09

I used to pee my bed because I didn't see the sense in going to the bathroom. Why waste the energy going to the bathroom and disturbing your sleep? They thought there was something wrong with me, but I just didn't understand their logic so I peed and slept soundly.

Not Proud

03/07/2004 at 15:37:00
Sometimes my house is so damned nasty I am afraid social services is going to come in here and shut down my life.

10/25/2000 at 19:08:05

I called my mom's cell phone when I was in my room so she could bring me dinner. My dad got pissed, so I called my mom and told her to tell him to fuck himself. Now my door's locked so my dad can't get in and I keep calling my mom to tell him to shut up.

Not Proud

10/04/2000 at 17:33:57
I've stopped using deodorant. No reason.

02/09/2003 at 22:36:50

Why is it that I can spend more than one hundred hours on a single video game when I can barely even put in five hours on my art? I care more about virtual killing than I do about actual living.

Not Proud

01/06/2004 at 03:13:43
Every day I miss another opportunity. I know where some of my talents lie and I neglect them. It's eating me up inside and I don't know if there's anything I can do about it. There are very few curses worse than potential.

12/13/2002 at 12:17:31
My tombstone will read, A LIFE NOT LIVED.

Gluttony

10/09/2000 at 14:18:06
I once ate a Skittle I found behind the toilet because it was a green one.

Not Proud

12/28/2000 at 15:49:33
I am more than an alcoholic. I am some kind of sick vodka-drinking-orgy-pervert.

02/24/2004 at 22:23:50
One time my mom made a cake, then left it for after dinner. I ate the whole thing, put the crumbs on the floor, rubbed them on the dog's face, and told everyone that the dog ate it.

Not Proud

02/26/2001 at 14:14:30
I love cheese. All kinds of cheese. I could cover everyone and everything with cheese and it still wouldn't be enough. Those *Tom and Jerry* episodes where Jerry is living inside a big wedge of Swiss cheese almost make me cry.

05/10/2004 at 10:55:24
I fried tofu in bacon fat.

Not Proud

11/11/2002 at 17:12:32
I used to eat huge amounts of food—ice cream, hamburgers, french fries, candy, cake frosting, cheese spread—and then vomit it all up. I would do this five times a day. Once I vomited into a bag in the car. I would go on dates and excuse myself to vomit. I wish I were bulimic again because I was very very thin and looked beautiful.

04/12/2004 at 08:20:16
When life sucks I eat a Twinkie.

Not Proud

09/10/2000 at 13:29:58
My favorite style of cuisine is all-you-can-eat. I set a mark of three full plates and I keep going until it's done. Feeling full isn't good enough for me. I just love to feast.

08/10/2002 at 06:18:11
I used to sell myself for heroin money.

Not Proud

12/01/2003 at 12:49:51
While eating dinner, I noticed the guy at the next table picking his nose. I handed him the oyster fork.

11/24/2002 at 11:36:32
I hate when people eat off my plate.

Not Proud

04/26/2004 at 23:50:02
I ate a box of cookies in a few minutes. They're the best cookies
I've ever eaten. They should call them "baked orgasms."

01/14/2001 at 20:39:38

Sometimes when I see people with emphysema wheeling around a tank of oxygen, it makes me wish I could wheel around a tank providing me with IV vodka tonics and a breathing tube thingy of beer. Also it would be nice to have an intermittent drip of Dilaudid, but I think that might be a bad idea in the long run.

Not Proud

12/05/2001 at 20:29:06
Ever eat a dozen eggs in one sitting? My head thought it was a tasty idea, but my stomach disagreed.

10/20/2003 at 14:11:48

I drank so much on Saturday night that I threw up four times the next a.m. And I was throwing up so hard that I popped some blood vessels in my eye and now half of my left eye is covered with blood. Not too sexy.

Not Proud

10/18/2000 at 04:30:54
I am a male bulimic and I do not know how to ask for help. I am ashamed because it is a disease of women.

12/19/2000 at 17:03:51
When I was a teenager I drank twelve sixteen-ounce bottles of
RC Cola just to see if I could win a prize in the fucking cap. I
won nothing and got diarrhea.

Not Proud

06/20/2001 at 03:34:41
I love to drink, and I love to play classical guitar. Unfortunately the two cannot coexist. It is a very sad thing.

05/05/2002 at 15:22:30
I was eating a box of doughnuts when a commercial for starving children in Ethiopia came on. Guilt is such a horrible emotion.

Not Proud

10/16/2000 at 23:54:47
I just put on my favorite coat from last year to walk the dog in
the cold. I found a pack of crackers and cheese that were in the
pocket from last March. They were good . . . aged cheese, you
know.

05/09/2003 at 19:49:58

Chex Mix, green olives, cheese and crackers, peanut butter and raspberry fruit spread, cheese sandwiches, Vicodin, French bread and butter. These are all my gross excesses. Being fat was one thing, but now I'm fat and stuck on painkillers. Not a good scene.

Not Proud

10/29/2003 at 14:44:23
When I don't drink it's impossible for me to pretend I'm happy
in my relationship.

02/16/2003 at 16:22:39
Every day, all day, is spent resisting eating.

Greed

02/22/2001 at 12:37:43
Whatever gets me what I want is good. Cheating, lying, and stealing are my tools.

Not Proud

12/23/2000 at 00:21:17
Anytime someone tries to give one of my friends attention, I automatically steal the spotlight away from them. I must be the center of attention. I must have all the love.

01/25/2002 at 15:05:03
For three years I worked as a receptionist at a church's office.
From the day I was hired to the day I left, I stole between four
hundred and five hundred dollars from the collection plate.

Not Proud

04/29/2004 at 05:15:07

I ate all of my kids' Easter eggs. Did I feel guilty? Of course I did. Did I regret it? Of course I did. Did I tell them that the Easter Bunny had to take the eggs back because too much chocolate makes you sick? Of course I did.

05/24/2002 at 07:26:53
When me and my girlfriend have had a little too much to drink . . . I wait till she has gone to the bathroom and steal money from her handbag. She never notices. "My round this time, honey."

Not Proud

02/17/2004 at 00:45:40
I don't like other people using the toilet at the office, so I locked the stall from the inside and posted an OUT OF ORDER sign on the front. When I need to launch a torpedo, I crawl under the door. The other day I heard someone say, "When are they gonna fix the toilet!" Shitting is a privilege for the smart. Dumbasses like my boss have to leave their logs at the restaurant across from the office.

04/19/2004 at 00:25:38
I charge interest whenever I lend my friends money, even if
they're broke.

Not Proud

01/21/2004 at 10:13:39
I steal batteries from work so I can use them in my vibrators.

06/11/2004 at 08:43:25
When I was really young, I went to a birthday party and we played pin the tail on the donkey. I cheated. They didn't put the blindfold on very good and I could see the donkey. I won some candy.

Not Proud

09/15/2000 at 12:37:17
I work in the accounts department of a major company and I steal things every day. Pens, paper clips, note pads, promo crap. I arrive ten minutes before anyone else and look around for some new stuff to "acquire." And I'm the first one to bitch when supplies are getting low.

11/24/2002 at 19:15:08
I emptied my daughter's piggy bank to buy a pack of cigarettes
and I feel shame.

Not Proud

12/14/2000 at 08:12:28
I've started working in an old-folks' home for the sole purpose
of getting my name into their wills. I am a horrible person, but
can't help myself.

04/17/2004 at 00:57:06

I make sixty-two thousand dollars a year and I bitch about not having enough money. Ten years ago when I made three hundred dollars a week, I used to hate people like myself that bitched about having no money yet made more than four thousand dollars a month. I really need to quit my job, and go cook again for ten bucks an hour to gain some perspective.

Not Proud

10/26/2000 at 17:48:22
I make sure I'm the banker in Monopoly so I can snag some
hundreds.

09/11/2000 at 19:39:44

Sometimes I have people over for dinner. When it comes time to serve the food I always serve myself just a little bit more. I don't know why. I just have to have the most.

Not Proud

10/16/2000 at 18:58:01
I take the bread out of the middle of the loaf and leave the smaller pieces and heels for other members of the family.

12/07/2000 at 13:47:48
Whenever somebody gives me too much change back, I never tell them. Ever.

Not Proud

11/13/2002 at 01:44:52

I steal money from my mom. In small enough amounts that she doesn't notice, but enough that it builds up. I like to think of it as payment for all the years she sent me to school without any food or money.

01/11/2001 at 15:01:43
When I had to do community service at the Salvation Army I found a dollar bill in the stuff I was sorting. I waited until no one was looking and pocketed it.

Not Proud

01/22/2001 at 23:58:49
I want a coworker to get fired so I can advance in my job. He's a nice guy, but he's in my way.

01/15/2002 at 09:36:34
I bum cigarettes off friends constantly. Although I'm a rather heavy smoker, I haven't bought a pack in months. If I'm going to get cancer, I want it to be on someone else's dime.

Not Proud

10/05/2000 at 01:32:33
I worked in the business of a friend for years and stole from
him daily.

04/14/2004 at 02:33:59

I really needed money for spring break. Luckily some old grandmother sent twenty dollars to the wrong house for her grandchild's birthday. Twenty dollars, gone on beer.

Not Proud

06/08/2003 at 22:45:20
I despise rich people, yet I aspire to be rich.

04/13/2004 at 16:59:18

Once I wanted to have birds as pets. So there was this nest, and I took the birds out and told my mom the cat ate them. All the baby birds died. I see the momma bird in my dreams. There is a place in hell for me.

Lust

02/24/2004 at 17:39:40
There was this girl I really liked in sixth grade and sometimes when I'm having sex, I accidentally say her name. I lose a lot of girlfriends that way.

Not Proud

06/17/2004 at 13:50:05
I don't think I'm with my soul mate. A soul mate would have way more sex with you.

12/16/2003 at 17:28:14

Today I was out walking the city with a couple of friends and we saw a black transsexual walk by. He/she was tall, thick, quite flamboyant, and a little cracked out. While my friends and everyone around us laughed and pointed at the freak, I kept quiet and admired his/her voluptuous ass in the tightest pair of jeans. Such rhythm in the way they walk. Living here, I see them all the time, and I want to fuck every one of them. They are sex addicts, and me, I am just insane.

Not Proud

03/20/2004 at 21:58:08
I slept with my secretary. Sorry, but he was really hot.

11/27/2003 at 04:07:01

I poked a hole in a condom and then had sex with my girl-friend. I got her pregnant and now we have a kid. I did this so I will never lose her and can continue having hot and sweaty sex with her.

Not Proud

02/13/2004 at 22:43:39
I am in lust with a married woman with two kids. I'm not ashamed to be a lesbian, but I am ashamed to be lusting after someone's mother and someone's wife.

10/13/2000 at 17:18:12

I cheated on my boyfriend with a friend's husband. He needed it, I needed it, and better he be with me than some stranger. No one need know. It was just one night. But the thought has crossed my mind . . . "His wedding ring has been inside of me."

Not Proud

03/20/2004 at 15:29:47
Clandestine activities. Car sex . . . good. Ass print on window . . . bad.

04/17/2004 at 14:09:21
I don't know if I love my girlfriend. I might; I might not. But I tell her I do so I can fuck her.

Not Proud

06/25/2003 at 08:21:01

You throw me down and bite my clothes off in the leaves, the mud, the water, the car, a table, any flat surface really—or not—against a wall, the floor, the kitchen counter, the women's bathroom sink, outside steps . . . ravenous unbridled passion. Just not the bedroom again.

10/11/2000 at 15:40:41
My friends and I bet for a free bar bill who can fuck the most overweight woman when we go out. It is not my fault that I always drink for free. They need to learn to bite the bullet and close their eyes.

Not Proud

10/06/2003 at 01:10:26
Once when my girl was giving me head, I slapped her across the face with it, just for the hell of it. She got pissed, so I said it was on accident. I figure the world needs guys like me, you know . . . to test the boundaries.

11/23/2003 at 20:26:10

I have an incomplete tarot card deck. It's missing a ton of cards. But I use it to give readings to girls, and when the cards are on the table, I interpret them to say whatever they need to say to get the girl in bed. I don't even know how to read them correctly.

Not Proud

11/26/2002 at 10:35:35
I cheated on my boyfriend with a guy who turned out to be a pedophile.

10/23/2002 at 21:44:27
My wife and I seduced her best friend into bed tonight. It was great sex and will probably ruin their friendship. They have been friends since grade school.

Not Proud

04/24/2003 at 23:21:50

I'm the good girl. I'm the 4.0 girl. I'm the artistic girl. I'm a parent's wet dream. And all I really want is to feel something. Something to let me know I'm still here, I'm alive. I want to be fucked up against a wall by a tall man with dark eyes and long-fingered hands. To be taken, to come and come again screaming, and not know his name. Sometimes I feel positively asexual. I want to be touched in the darkness.

04/19/2004 at 08:50:51
I swallowed cum for the first time yesterday. Now he is forever inside me.

Not Proud

04/13/2004 at 00:58:15
I love it when he wakes me up with his fingers. I don't trust you
with my heart yet, boy, but at least for now I'll let you play with
my body . . . you're damn good at it.

02/17/2003 at 23:17:50
Sex has been the cornerstone of every one of my functional
relationships.

Not Proud

09/06/2002 at 23:46:04

I'm a horny college guy. Almost every other night I'm at a bar or a frat party picking up some random girl, going home with her . . . and, well . . . having sex with her. I've probably had sex with almost thirty to fifty women since last Christmas. It's just so easy. What I don't tell them is that virtually every one I've gone home with I've given herpes to.

10/27/2000 at 20:31:26
I go to the adult bookstore and let other guys watch me jerk off
in the window booths. My wife thinks I love her.

Not Proud

06/09/2003 at 00:30:10
Although you're half a planet away from me, and while I have a
family of my own and we're not friends anymore, I still smell
your sweat on me.

03/26/2004 at 23:03:16
There's this guy who I find repulsive, but I am considering doing it with him simply because I am horny and there's something erotic and dirty about getting it on with someone so unappealing.

Not Proud

03/29/2002 at 17:54:25
My girlfriend left me when I asked her to pretend we were
cousins whilst having sex.

11/29/2000 at 20:44:57
I like to cheat on my boyfriend with really ugly fucking guys.
That way, if he ever hears about anything, I just deny it and say,
"Baby, why would I cheat on a great guy like you with someone
so ugly?" He falls for that line every time.

Not Proud

10/08/2000 at 15:13:53
I am usually only attracted to married men and priests. I didn't ask for it to be this way, that's just the way it is. I also ran over a dog once.

11/07/2001 at 16:54:42
I was looking out the window waiting for the pizza man when
my husband came up behind me and asked for a quickie. I said
sure as long as he could do it while I looked out the window. He
fucked me from behind while I watched children jumping rope
in the parking lot.

Not Proud

12/14/2003 at 02:32:58
It has come to my attention that having anal sex on the first date will not make me some guy's dream girl and future wife. Dammit.

11/04/2003 at 15:00:46

I once slept with my philosophy professor. . . . I feel no guilt, but everyone thinks I did it for the grade. I was already acing the class. If I did it for the grade I would have slept with my calculus prof instead.

Not Proud

12/13/2000 at 20:16:01
I like pornography more than sex.

12/13/2001 at 01:24:19
I was always getting in trouble in preschool for rubbing myself during naptime and playing doctor with the other kids.

Not Proud

06/26/2002 at 13:40:43
The night I impregnated my wife, I was fantasizing about her sister.

10/18/2002 at 02:06:44
Our cat has watched us fuck.

Not Proud

02/22/2002 at 04:54:15
When I was eleven I found a chest full of my dad's personal stuff. It had an amateur nude photo of my mom from before I was born. I took it out and licked it.

11/22/2002 at 18:57:37
I like to walk in the park at night and fondle the statues.

Not Proud

02/23/2001 at 23:46:28
I like to see girls jump.

02/08/2002 at 13:25:34
I have coveted my neighbor's wife—several times a week for the past sixteen years.

Not Proud

02/21/2001 at 17:32:06
Remember your first kiss? I've never had one.

10/04/2000 at 23:49:38
I filled up my four-gig hard drive with porn pictures. Mostly of pregnant ethnic women.

Not Proud

12/30/2001 at 21:33:03

I cheat on my husband all the time. He doesn't see me as anything to worry about, so I keep doing it. He never knows or cares . . . yet sometimes he will come in and fuck me when I am sleeping. This is the only time we will ever have sex . . . weird.

04/23/2002 at 21:07:14
I faked it every time.

Not Proud

03/06/2004 at 23:47:37
She's married, and a truly great friend. I want to fuck her for all
the right reasons, all the wrong, and a few others I don't even
know how to categorize.

02/09/2004 at 19:38:00
Right now what I really want is an unhealthy, screwed up, overly sexed relationship.

Not Proud

07/31/2002 at 17:03:44
I am married and very much bisexual. My husband knows I like
women, but he doesn't know I love them.

04/20/2003 at 23:56:59

I fooled around with your husband. He's really small down there or else I would have had sex with him too. Now I see you all the time and I smile and give you a kiss, with the same mouth that sucked your husband's cock.

Not Proud

01/27/2004 at 04:01:13
I spunked in my friend's aquarium and the fish ate it. I love all fish. Especially the little pink ones. They are my bitches.

Anger

10/12/2000 at 17:28:17
I find violence more and more appealing as a way to solve petty differences and problems.

Not Proud

01/01/2004 at 03:35:31
If you tell me one more fuckin' story about what your cats did on the weekend, I'm going to kill them with a rusty weed whacker and mail you their remains.

04/26/2004 at 14:19:27

I'm planning to kill my boyfriend. I like him, but he asks too many questions. He's going to find out eventually and I can't let him tell anyone. It's amazing how easy it all seems. Have to learn more about poisons though.

Not Proud

04/22/2004 at 03:08:11

I'm a guy and I wish I could wear fur just to piss off all of those animal activists. Of course fur doesn't suit me, so I'll just keep hunting game while driving my leather upholstered gas guzzling SUV to the steakhouse. Perhaps I could have my SUV reupholstered in fur.

01/02/2004 at 14:53:42
I love going to the hardware store. Going up and down the aisles fantasizing over the different tools to kill you with. I spent fifteen minutes in the hammer section alone.

Not Proud

05/18/2004 at 15:40:29
My neighbor's terrier woke me up again. Barked until three a.m. I made a voodoo doll of the dog and stuck pins in its neck. I just found out it needs an operation to remove a throat polyp. I didn't know voodoo worked on animals.

02/24/2004 at 03:15:38

Four years ago a guy stole my girlfriend. My girl and I patched things up, but a month ago I fucked his fiancée. The night before the wedding. Revenge is best served cold.

Not Proud

05/02/2004 at 22:38:51
My liver is so pissed off at me.

07/07/2002 at 21:15:35
I secretly hate one of my friends, so when he passed out at a party I drew a swastika on his forehead in black permanent marker.

Not Proud

03/31/2004 at 20:44:21

I've begun yelling at my kids out of frustration again. I need to stop doing that because it just hurts them and really does nothing to make me feel better. I know that if I keep this up, ten years from now when they're teenagers, they're just going to resent me as the crotchety old motherfucker that I really am. My kids already respect me without me yelling at them, I don't know why I do it. You know you've got a problem when your three-year-old little girl looks at you and says, "Daddy, settle down."

05/02/2004 at 17:24:40
I actually looked into hiring an assassin to kill your fiancé. I
wanted to be close enough to see your face when he died.

Not Proud

04/12/2004 at 21:42:11

God does not deserve to be worshipped. He pisses me off so damn much for existing and having the power to end all of this shit and make everyone happy, yet he doesn't. I don't know why everyone expects him to give them a great afterlife when he obviously can't deliver in this one.

01/25/2004 at 20:27:28

I read that when the Romans didn't like you they used to throw you over a cliff. Like a sack of garbage. If my boss lived back then he would have been the first one to hit the rocks. Shit, I would throw him over myself if they gave me the chance and hope he just breaks something so the birds and animals have something to feed on for a few days.

Not Proud

08/14/2002 at 08:47:17
I really and truly love my boyfriend but sometimes I just want
to crack him on the head with a brick. Like, twice.

07/08/2003 at 20:41:31

I am angry at my stepdaughter's anorexia/bulimia and the cavalier way she looks at it. I am angry at the crap that she writes on her arms, legs, and her back for that matter, and thinks nothing of it. I am angry that I cannot look past that shaved head and ridiculous clothing she wears. I am angry that my wife can look past it all and say, "If that is what she wants to do, let her," and I can't. I am angry that I am intolerant.

Not Proud

10/10/2000 at 14:20:20
I just farted inside this one asshole's coffee mug at work. It's the closest I can get to having him eat shit.

07/10/2002 at 21:30:48
Over the past few years I've made out a hit list of people who have either hurt me, judged me, angered me, or anything like that. There's about two hundred people on it. And I dearly wish to kill every single one of them. The hit list is just for alleviation . . . but the hate is real.

Not Proud

06/09/2003 at 16:22:27

Mom . . . why won't you do anything? Dad beats me . . . and you just leave me all alone with him. I know you think I'm the worst daughter . . . but can't you help me a little? I hope my bruises haunt you in your dreams.

06/29/2003 at 01:30:20
I hate my husband for making me believe that there's no such thing as a soul mate and that romantic love is a scam. I hate him and really ought to stop fucking him, but I need him to help raise our kids.

Not Proud

06/17/2004 at 03:49:12
I hate the fact that I got a disease when I lost my virginity.

11/11/2002 at 15:47:07
A friend of mine stole three hundred dollars of my graduation money. I confronted her about it. She never paid me back. So, I have tried to make up three hundred dollars' worth of fat jokes about her. It's hard to judge the exact value of them, though.

Not Proud

03/14/2002 at 02:42:34
When I was about ten years old, my younger sister had a pet budgie that never stopped chirping and always used to annoy the crap out of me. One day it bit me, and I threw it into its cage, head first. The next day it was dead. No one knows it was me.

12/19/2003 at 22:56:28
Frankly, the most pleasurable present I could get this Christmas
is a set a brass knuckles to punch my boyfriend in the face with.

Not Proud

01/31/2002 at 13:58:25
I'm an attractive girl, and this guy was standing really, REAL-
LY close up to me in the art museum while I was looking at the
art, so I farted.

01/20/2002 at 08:00:49
I place fake obituaries in the local newspaper of people who annoy me.

Not Proud

02/22/2001 at 16:43:08
To whoever stole my watch at the gym yesterday, I sincerely hope you die of syphilis.

10/11/2000 at 14:59:04
My girlfriend cheated on me with a cop. I went to a hunting store and bought a bottle of deer urine. I poured it in the heater vent of his patrol car. I understand that the city is going to declare his car a total loss. Seems they can't get the smell out.

Not Proud

10/12/2000 at 09:30:41
I was so angry in traffic this morning that I wished that there were limbs or something scattered all over the road to explain the congestion.

03/05/2004 at 14:35:17

I was at the mall the other day and this lady was really rude to me in the office-supply aisle. When she was digging through file folders, mumbling to herself, I opened a jar of india ink and poured it down the back of her little girl's pink dress. I then went to another store where I got the shit I needed on sale anyway.

Not Proud

03/05/2001 at 10:23:17
I told my best friend, who then passed it around to everyone at work, that my ex-boyfriend, who works for the same company, only has one testicle.

10/04/2000 at 20:44:54
I put poison ivy on my ex-husband's underwear so he would
think he had a disease.

Not Proud

01/01/2002 at 06:56:16

I fucked this guy out of spite, self-pity, stupidity, and all because I hate my boyfriend when I'm drunk. Easier to hate him than to admit it's me I hate.

10/06/2000 at 19:04:55

Somebody ate my lunch today—right out of the fridge at work. Unfortunately for that sorry bastard somebody's been stealing my lunch a lot. And today, whoever stole my lunch had a cat-food sandwich! Ha, ha, ha! You freakin' loser. How was it?! Good, I hope! I think it was my boss.

Not Proud

04/09/2003 at 18:13:01

I hate my mother to such a degree none of you reading this could possibly comprehend it. Does your mother annoy you, nag you, beat you, screw your boyfriend? Big deal. Cope. The shadow of my mother makes Satan crap his pants.

Misc.

06/11/2004 at 22:05:08
I got a dog for the sole purpose of blaming my farts on him.

Not Proud

10/04/2000 at 17:04:42
I wanted to laugh when I found out my boss had cancer.

04/03/2003 at 13:19:00

I memorized what type of shoes most people in my department wear, so I know who is taking a shit at any given time. What a waste of a photographic memory. . . .

Not Proud

04/06/2004 at 17:53:43
One time when I was ten, I shot the little neighbor girl in the neck with my BB gun while she wasn't looking. I was pretending I was a sniper. I feel really bad because she started crying and nobody ever found out that I did it.

02/24/2004 at 22:02:17
My computers see more of me than my friends and family.

Not Proud

10/04/2000 at 15:32:08
One time my grandmother got up from her chair and I smelled the cushions.

04/10/2001 at 16:13:21

Last year at my friend's birthday party I put half a fifth of vodka into the family's prized fifty-five-gallon saltwater aquarium. All the fish died and I found out that his mom had spent, like, ten years perfecting the perfect aquamarine setup. I felt like an asshole and I wasted a lot of perfectly good vodka too.

Not Proud

12/19/2000 at 15:27:29
I like to sit in my bathroom late at night when I think my room-mate is asleep and make animal and baby noises while I take a crap.

09/26/2002 at 13:09:19

I have only once loved a person I actually know. I dream about celebrities. Right now I'm madly in love with a football player who has a great Web site that I visit daily. Ordinary people suck.

Not Proud

05/31/2003 at 14:32:25
My parents died eighteen months apart of the same disease.
When people ask me what they died of I don't tell the truth
because I'll look like an idiot and feel so guilty. They died of
lung cancer and I am still a smoker.

01/07/2004 at 21:09:56
Sometimes I confuse confidence with a loud voice. Often I mistake exhaustion for depression. Though I am not an idiot, I generally have no freakin' idea what the hell is going on around me.

Not Proud

03/31/2004 at 22:34:25
My diary looks like a giant suicide note.

05/13/2003 at 21:12:41

I once was cleaning out my fish tank with one of those suction hose devices and I accidentally sucked out the eyeball of one my goldfishes. It lived and is still today swimming around with a giant hollowed out hole in the side of its head.

Not Proud

11/13/2002 at 01:21:51
I want to hurt other people. Not in the bashing-heads sort of way, but in the cruel emotional sense. It's the only kick I get anymore.

11/28/2001 at 12:36:57
I dumped a guy once because I hated his voice. He was VERY
good looking, but when you're in a long-distance relationship,
a voice really does count for a lot.

Not Proud

04/14/2002 at 02:31:53
I burned down my house when I was a kid. The fire marshal said the fire started in the wiring, but I know that I left a fire going under my bed just a couple of minutes before my parents pulled me out of the house.

11/28/2000 at 18:41:22

One time I farted in a jar of pennies. I placed the lid back on and waited a few minutes. Then I took the lid off and inhaled deeply. It smelled like fart mixed with metal. I giggled for close to five minutes. I'm twenty-five years old and possess a high degree of intelligence.

Not Proud

10/29/2002 at 18:51:05
I am struggling to forgive the guy who fed heroin to my son,
which killed him.

04/29/2003 at 03:35:01

There was a boy about the same age as me who died while I was in junior high. I didn't know him too well, but I was very close friends with his cousin. The day after his death my friend stayed in the halls during school. I stayed with him and we talked. At one point I wished someone would die more often.

Not Proud

05/07/2002 at 11:01:34
It really upsets me that I lost the vision of your face.

06/26/2001 at 11:39:52
Whenever I see a dead pigeon or other bird, I like to pick it up
and give it a proper burial. Sometimes I cremate them.

Not Proud

04/18/2004 at 04:59:12
I killed my girlfriend's dog because it bit me once. She cried because she thought it got hit by a car . . . and it did . . . my car.

01/16/2003 at 03:43:20

Well, it took me a long time to finally realize, but I am gay. I hated the thought of it—being a gay man was pretty much the worst thing a man could be when I was growing up. I've never had a girlfriend; I get nervous when a guy strips or pees around me. (Because I have an instinct to look, and I know in my mind he'll notice and think I'm gay.) And also, the dreams I've had of masturbating another man. It all points to one conclusion and I can now admit it. I feel at peace. I am going to tell everyone, and I don't think most will be surprised. Also, I've had a lot of anger and prejudice. I hated gay people. I was so repressed, I had to try to hate it so I would not become it. But I am sick and tired and I'm just going to be what I was meant to be. I am gay.

Not Proud

01/18/2001 at 15:53:47
I have hair on my back, and in this country/society, that feels worse than being a serial rapist, Nazi, child killer, child actor . . .

10/08/2000 at 00:45:52
I'm a twenty-eight-year-old guy and I still sleep with a teddy bear. I just can't give it up. If my girlfriend and/or relatives ever find out, I could just kill myself instead of facing the embarrassment.

Not Proud

10/08/2000 at 11:34:05
I like to sing in my living room like I'm in front of a bunch of people.

11/05/2003 at 00:15:30
I married your juicy brain and your wicked sense of humor, but
I've never longed for your body. I love you, but you're hideous.

Not Proud

12/07/2000 at 19:51:41

After I have oral sex with my girlfriend, I enjoy smelling her vagina on my breath. Someone should write a song about that.

10/13/2000 at 14:46:10
I take a sick pleasure in reading other people's miseries.

Scott Huot is a writer and artist from Montreal, Quebec. He is also a senior Web content producer for a motion picture effects software company.

GW Brazier is a writer and musician, also from Montreal. He is creative director of Blue Dot Communications Inc., an award-winning digital media firm.

CUSTOMS & ETIQUETTE OF
THAILAND

Derek Tonkin &
Visnu Kongsiri

Customs & Etiquette of Thailand
by Derek Tonkin & Visnu Kongsiri

First published 1990 by Global Books Ltd.
Second edition 1996, Third edition 1998
This edition published 2005 by
Simple Guides an imprint of Bravo Ltd.
59 Hutton Grove
London N12 8DS
Tel: +44 (0) 208 446 2440
Fax: +44 (0) 208 446 2441
Enquiries: office@kuperard.co.uk
www.kuperard.co.uk

© 2005 Bravo Ltd.
Reprinted 2006

ISBN-13: 978-1-85733-396-1
ISBN-10: 1-85733-396-9

British Library Cataloguing in Publication Data
A CIP catalogue entry for this book
is available from the British Library

Cover image: ©Simon Reddy / www.travel-ink.co.uk
Set in Futura 11 on 12 pt by Bookman, Hayes
Printed and bound in China

Contents

Preface

The original 1990 edition of this book, entitled *Simple Etiquette in Thailand*, was written by Derek Tonkin, shortly after he returned to London, following a very successful period as British Ambassador in Bangkok from 1986-89. On publication, the book was very positively reviewed by the Thai press. Indeed, it reflected the author's great sensitivity and insight into the culture and language of the Thai people that was so widely appreciated during his term as Ambassador.

To be asked, therefore, by the new publishers, Global Books Ltd, to collaborate with the publication of a revised and expanded new edition was certainly something of a challenge; but also a great privilege. There was so little of the original that required any kind of change; it was more a question of what to add and update where I could in the hope of making the new edition fully reflective of Thai culture and traditions in the last decade of the twentieth century. I hope this has been achieved satisfactorily.

In this third edition, I have had the opportunity to add further updates and clarifications, together with important new sections on Funerals, Markets and Facts About Thailand, plus a revised mini Vocabulary. I write at a difficult time for the Thai economy although a more advantageous time for Western visitors in particular. Nevertheless, Thai customs and our way of life remain timeless and I believe our hospitality continues to be one of our singular virtues.

VISNU KONGSIRI

MAP OF THAILAND

1

The Land

Royal Palace

We used to know Thailand as 'Siam'. The country changed its name in 1939, reverted to Siam again for a brief period after the Second World War, but changed back permanently to Thailand in 1949.

NOTE: 'Thailand' was devised just before the Second World War when Thai nationalism was particularly strong. Most scholars say that the term 'Siam' (possibly related to 'Shan' – Shan States in Burma) was a word originally used by Thailand's neighbours (Chinese, Burmese, Khmers) to describe Thailand. But some scholars have recently argued that Siam is, after all, a good Thai word.

The Thais themselves have called their country, in their own language, 'Thai-land' (*muang thai*, more formally *prathet thai*) for many centuries but Siam (*sayam*) has also been used as the formal name as well. Thailand, which means literally 'Land of the Free', is now the only correct international name, but Siam still appears in royal titles and in the names of some banks, companies and newspapers.

Thailand's neighbours include *Myanmar* (Burma) to the West, Laos to the North, Cambodia to East and Malaysia to the South. Thailand, situated in the Tropic of Cancer, is about the size of France but has a population of about 60 million. There are four main regions: the North – mountainous, cool in the winter and home to numerous hill tribes; the North-East – an arid plateau bordered to the East by the River Mekong; the Central Plains – a fertile rice-growing region around Bangkok; and the South – rich in rubber, tin and lush vegetation and also home to the majority of Thai Muslims.

Visitors to Thailand should be aware of a unique feature of the country's history: it was never colonized by any Western country. Over the centuries the Thais did battle with their neighbours, notably the Burmese and the Khmers (Cambodians). But from the thirteenth century onwards the Thais created a nation-state which has survived intact to this day. Thailand came under some pressure from Western trading nations in the seventeenth century. Two centuries later, during the hey-day of colonial expansionism, the British in Burma and Malaya and the French in Laos and

Cambodia secured significant concessions in territory as well as trade. But the Thais, under the wise leadership of King Mongkut (Rama IV), 1851–68, and King Chulalongkorn (Rama V), 1868–1910, succeeded where almost all other South-East Asian nations failed, in preserving their independence.

The absence of a colonial past (though Thailand made sensible use of the services of numerous Western advisers, particularly from France, Britain and Germany) is important to an understanding of Thai mentality. Visitors are welcomed as equals. Racial and religious prejudice is virtually unknown. Buddhist tolerance goes hand-in-hand with intense national pride. However, regional economic problems have slowed down growth considerably, and the *de facto* devaluation of the Thai Baht in late 1997, although benefiting the tourist, has forced the Government to institute many belt-tightening measures. Thailand has the natural and human resources both to enjoy the benefits of industrialization and to preserve its traditions and culture, blessed as it is with an economy balanced between light industry, agriculture and services.

NOTE: In 1782 the crown was offered to one of King Tak Sin's generals, Chao Phraya Chakri, who was crowned with the title of Rama I. The present monarch is HM King Bhumibol Adulyadej, the ninth monarch in the Chakri Dynasty, or Rama IX. (Many Thai Kings have used the name 'Rama', derived from the name of the hero of the Indian epic Ramayana. Rama was the archetype of the perfect ruler. The system of designating monarchs in the present Chakri dynasty as 'Rama' was created by King Vajiravudh, who became Rama VI. He renamed all previous monarchs Rama I–V).

Thailand's principal exports have been rice, rubber, manioc and canned goods, but in recent years manufactured products have overtaken traditional agricultural produce and include jewellery, integrated circuits, textiles and footwear. Thailand now exports bicycles to Britain and television sets to Germany.

Overseas visitors, especially those from the West, are known to the Thais as *farangs*. The word is most probably a corruption of 'Frank' and originally meant Caucasians from the ports of the Near East (and not 'French', as popularly believed, although the Thai word for France is *farang-saet*). It is also the Thai word for the guava fruit. As a *guava/farang* in Thailand, you can never escape your Western origins. Yet there are, inevitably, those earnest young Westerners on a longish stay in Thailand who desperately wish to assimilate and become indistinguishable from their Thai hosts. One has to wonder why. As a six-foot, blue-eyed Scandinavian, you are never going to merge with the local Thai population. The Thais much prefer you as you are!

THAI ROYAL FAMILY

There are two institutions of which every visitor to Thailand should be aware. First, the Monarchy. The Thai Royal Family holds a very special place in the hearts of all Thai people, from the farmer working in his rice field to the head of an international business empire sitting behind his desk in a modern office building. You will find portraits of Their Majesties and other members of the Royal Family displayed prominently in every home and office. This is done not because of some personality cult as in a number of socialist countries, but because of the genuine love and respect that the Thai people have for the Royal Family, especially the present King who has devoted his entire life to improving the well-being of his subjects.

Any disrespect shown to Their Majesties, either by word or deed, will be met with a very strong reaction and could land you in real trouble. There was a story once about a foreign entertainment editor of a local English language newspaper who suggested keeping emergency money in your socks when going for a night out. But because Thai bank notes have an image of the King on them, this raised howls of protest and he had to issue an apology and retraction.

The King has a special anthem, called the Royal Anthem, which is played whenever he or his representative arrives or leaves a function or ceremony. It is also played when a toast is made to His Majesty's health. Although it is not the same as the National Anthem, it is given the same respect and you should stand up.

RESPECT FOR BUDDHIST RELIGION

The second institution of special importance in Thailand is the Buddhist religion for Buddhism is the major guiding influence of the Thai people. Behave modestly and sensibly in all matters concerning the Buddhist religion, especially when visiting temples. Always take your shoes off when entering the *Bot*, where the main Buddha image is housed and where the major ceremonies, such as ordination, take place. Remember to step over the door threshold (a raised horizontal piece of wood at the bottom of the entrance) as it is considered disrespectful to step on it. Do be careful, too, about taking photographs inside a temple. There may be restrictions. As regards the proper behaviour for women towards monks, see section on Visiting Temples (pp.67-8).

Buddha images, no matter how large or small, how old or new, are considered sacred. This is because they pass through various ceremonies performed by senior monks. (Those that you see in shops around the Giant Swing near Wat Sutat are for sale and have not yet gone through these ceremonies.) Because they are sacred, you should not use them for decoration in homes or offices. There are also very strict laws governing the export of Buddha images and you should make sure that all documents are in order before attempting to do so.

2

The People

'Buddhism is the major guiding influence'[*]

Thailand was settled over the centuries by waves of migration, including Khmers and Mons (from Burma) and various peoples from southern China. The Thais arrived from Yunnan in southern China in the tenth and eleventh centuries and by the thirteenth century had established the first Thai capital at Sukhothai, moving to Ayutthaya in the fourteenth century and to Bangkok in the eighteenth century.

Most Thais live in the countryside. A typical rural family will include grandparents, cousins, an uncle or aunt, even children of distant relatives. Living together under one roof encourages natural courtesy, tolerance and mutual respect, in the interests of social harmony. Urban households retain these traditional values, as far as practicable; invariably, there are relatives up-country and so most urban Thais retain, and enjoy, their links with the countryside.

From an early age, Thais are brought up to accept a code of social behaviour based on respect for superiors, parents, teachers and the elderly. Accordingly, the emphasis in relationships tends to be vertical, rather than horizontal; deference, avoidance of conflict, a desire to please, are hallmarks of the Thai character. This has in the past encouraged patronage and somewhat limited the scope for advancement by merit. But as Thailand progresses economically and a sophisticated, urbanized population emerges, opportunities for personal advancement, particularly in the private sector, are increasing rapidly.

UNDERSTANDING BUDDHISM

The Buddhist religion has been a dominant influence, probably the most important factor, in the development of the Thai personality. Thai village life over the years has followed a cyclical pattern of farming which is reflected in a cycle of fixed Buddhist festivals throughout the year. Buddhism is a religion of simplicity and quiet contemplation. The Buddha, which means simply 'The Enlightened One,' was a prince who lived in Northern India 25 centuries ago (add 543 to the Western year to obtain the Buddhist year; AD1998, therefore, becomes BE2541 [Buddhist Era] in Thailand); he renounced material comforts in the search for enlightenment about the nature of human existence. In Thailand, Buddhism was enhanced by Brahminism, which brought colour, festivity and ritual to the religion and gave the Thai people a pleasantly practical interpretation of the Buddha's teachings.

On the whole, Thais are content to accept their lot without carping or resentment, though their approach to life is invariably positive, carefree and good-natured. There is perhaps a certain fatalism in their attitude, deriving from the Buddhist concept of 'karma,' which basically means 'action': the law under which your present life is determined by the cumulative merit of previous existences, and good deeds in this life will be reflected in your next life. Although materialist influences have in recent years had some impact, most Thais prefer a life of contentment and enjoyment to one of material acquisition.

Buddhism teaches that life is suffering, that earthly pleasures are only transient and that progress towards enlightenment and the attainment of eventual 'nirvana' (salvation) requires personal commitment. The acquisition of merit through good deeds helps to this end. Thais do not believe, however, that life should be taken all that seriously. As farmers, Thais know that rice cultivation is strenuous work and that life would not be all that much fun without some diversion and communal jollity. Ploughing, seeding, transplantation and harvesting would certainly be tedious without having a laugh. Work and play do indeed mix in Thailand, so much so that the word for work, *ngarn*, is also the word for festival or fair; the common meaning is communality.

Top Tip: *Sanuk* – Having Fun

One of the first words you will learn in Thai is *sanuk* (pronounced sa-nook), which roughly translated means fun. No activity in Thailand is thought worth undertaking unless it is *sanuk*. When a friend tells you what he has been up to, you are almost expected to ask '*Sanuk mai?*' or 'Was it fun?' The Thai life-style, whether in the town or country, is geared to pleasurable activities. A night out with friends, a trip up-country, a visit to relatives, a walk to a temple at festival times will all be *sanuk*.

As activity frequently involves travel, another essential Thai expression is *bpai tiao* (pronounced by-tiaow, as in 'miaow'), which literally means 'to go on a trip'; we would say 'going out'. Thais love to travel, whether short or longish journeys, since travel involves socializing, seeing new faces, meeting up with old friends. An evening at the cinema, a walk across the fields, a visit to a fair, are typical examples of *bpai tiao* which can also include chatting up girls and a night out on the town. *Bpai tiao* is, by definition, almost certain to be *sanuk*.

Brahmani 'spirit shrine'

SPIRIT WORLD

Another strong influence on the Thais is the unknown, the supernatural, the world of spirits. Thais have a strong sense of the inexplicable, an acute awareness of the mystery of nature. The clearest manifestation of this are the gaily-coloured spirit houses which grace most gardens and households and places of natural beauty, or ominous interest like an outcrop of rocks near a temple, or an accident-prone locality on a high-way. The local guardian spirits are there by natural right; people are only incidental occupants of land and property and need to respect, and occasion-ally humour, the local spirits.

In daily life, many Thais take care not to upset the spirits who are thought to be born out of the souls of departed human beings. Some spirits are perceived more as ghosts (called *pee*), unpredictable and malevolent, the source of misfortune and chicanery, the cause of terror, illness and material loss. In north-east Thailand, spirit worship is especially active.

It is scarcely surprising that, in such an uncertain world, Thais take sensible precautions. As a basic rule of conduct, no human venture should be launched until the auspicious moment has arrived. No business undertaking is initiated, no marriage solemnized, no decision of substance taken until the precise time designated by astrological calculation has been reached. An invitation to the opening of a new branch office, for example, will indicate in the programme the precise minute at which the new venture will be most auspiciously launched.

Dreams, premonitions, intuitive knowledge are taken seriously. Good and bad omens are seen as portents of success and failure. Charms and amulets are worn by many Thais, the most popular type of amulet naturally being small images of the Buddha. Spells and incantations, mystic formulae and protective tattoos all help to subdue malevolent spirits, who can also be bribed to remain dormant or, temporarily, go away.

After all, since whatever you do and whatever precautions you may take may not achieve the desired result, it is better not to worry. *Mai bpen rai* or 'never mind' is heard on almost any occasion. Literally it means 'there isn't anything' and it is a bit like the French *ce n'est rien* and the German *macht nichts*. *Mai bpen rai*, however, is used so much more frequently than equivalent Western expressions that it suggests as much a state of mind, an extension of Buddhist philosophy and, to the Westerner, sounds even a little exasperating.

> ## Top Tip: Relax in Times of Adversity!
>
> Thais have learnt to relax in times of adversity and disappointment. They do not get over-excited, for example, if the train is late or if they are stuck in a traffic-jam on the way to the airport. No need to cry; better to laugh instead.

FAMILY STRUCTURE

The basic social structure in Thailand is the individual family; groups of families are associated in village communities. The family represents stability and security in an ever-changing, uncertain world. Loyalty to and respect for the family, to the village, to the monarchy and to the country are highly developed. This encourages a strong sense of national identity and pride.

Family ties are of the utmost importance in Thailand, and this is reflected in the specific title given to each relative. For instance, is Aunt Mary your father's younger or older sister? In

Thailand you can tell immediately by the designation given to her. Some of the more important designations for relatives are as follows:

pee	— Elder brother or sister
nong	— Younger brother or sister
phoo	— Paternal grandfather
yah	— Paternal grandmother
dhah	— Maternal grandfather
yaai	— Maternal grandmother
loong	— Elder brother of father or mother
bhah	— Elder sister of father or mother
ah	— Younger brother or sister of father
nah	— Younger brother or sister of mother

However, these designations are often used colloquially for people who are completely unrelated. For instance, a young waiter or waitress may be called over to your table by using the designation *nong*.

VISITING THAI HOMES

Despite the emphasis on eating out in Thailand, you may occasionally be invited to a Thai home. Even in modern apartments, the rule is to take off your shoes. It is mainly a token of respect and not so much a desire, as Westerners tend to assume, not to bring dirt into the household; it is also much cooler without shoes on. You will probably sit on chairs, but you might also be invited to sit on the floor. Try not to sit cross-legged; sit on your heels if you wish; better still, tuck your legs under you on one side, supporting yourself if you must with one hand. Try not to sit against a wall with your feet pointing out.

GIFTS

Take a small present for your host, who may give you one in return. Flowers are always welcome, or a box of local confectionary/cookies, or some attractive small ornament: it need not be large and expensive. It is the thought that counts. Thais themselves love presents; they are often beautifully wrapped with pretty ribbon. It used to be thought bad form to open presents straight away, but this taboo is less strict nowadays and, if invited, you may take a look. On balance, though, it is better to put the present aside until later, unless you are quite sure it would not cause offence by opening it up there and then.

If you are staying overnight, spare a thought for the house spirits. There is in particular the Lord of the Place (Phra Phum) who has his shrine in the compound and there are possibly other spirits of the locality, normally at least another eight. I once slept*, unawares, in a room haunted by a malevolent spirit, but as I was a foreigner, I had nothing to worry about.

---

* Co-author Derek Tonkin

24

3

Social Relations

Traditional 'figure-nail' dance

Thais are very sociable. You will find it fun (*sanuk*) getting to know them. But before doing so, you should try to learn something about their social codes.

GREETING

Thais greet each other very much as people do anywhere else in the world, with a cheery sign of recognition and a chat. The most usual greeting (and also a farewell), appropriate on almost all occasions, is *sawatdee* which literally means 'May you prosper'. It may be used at any time of the day or night. To be polite, men should add the word *krap* and women the word *ka*, so that for men it is *sawatdee krap* and for women *sawatdee ka*. *Krap* (in Bangkok often shortened to *k'ap*) and *ka*, incidentally, are the nearest words you can get in Thai to 'yes,' though they mean little more than 'I hear you'. You can also say *sabai dee*, which is closer to our 'How are you?', but not so frequent as *sawatdee* except in the north-east (and Laos).

Thais do not normally shake hands among themselves, though they will shake Western hands because they know that is what foreigners do. Custom, however, is slowly changing and in recent years it has become accepted practice for Thais to shake hands among themselves on special occasions, for example, when signing commercial contracts or at prize-givings, particularly at sports meetings, where both a *wai* and a handshake are in order. However, do not be put off if a Thai lady seems reluctant to shake hands as this is quite normal since physical contact between strangers of the opposite sex is not considered proper.

THE *WAI*

The traditional Thai greeting, and farewell, is to raise both hands gracefully and unhurriedly, palm to palm, fingers together, and close to the body, in what is known as the *wai* (pronounced 'why'). Your fingertips should be between your chin and the top of your nose, but never higher than your eyes, unless the *wai* is directed at a Buddha image or the King. It is tempting, but mistaken, to regard this as the equivalent of our handshake. In Thailand, to *wai* means not only to greet and to say farewell; more importantly, it means to pay your respects. Therefore you will see Thais giving a *wai* when they pass shrines or the statue of a respected King. The higher you raise your hands and the lower you bend your head, the greater the respect you wish to convey. A *wai* must always be acknowledged. This is normally done with another *wai*, but a nod or a smile is usually sufficient for children or those of lower status.

The '*wai*'

The *wai* is accordingly always initiated by the person whose status, for reasons of age or rank, is inferior to the person to whom respects are being paid. When you join your Thai International flight at London, Frankfurt, Sydney, Los Angeles, or wherever, the exquisitely dressed Thai air hostess will always *wai* to you, and she will *wai* to you again when you leave the flight in Bangkok. She does not expect you to respond; a smile and a nod are all that is needed. When you arrive at your hotel, you are likely to be met with another *wai* as you enter. Again, do not try to respond; it is not expected and you will be at a loss about how to *wai* with your hands full of luggage.

A person who initiates a *wai* is likely to bend his head to a greater or lesser extent, depending on the status of the person receiving the *wai*. Note how members of the Thai Royal Family at religious ceremonies themselves *wai* to the Buddhist clergy and how the latter, because of their special status in society, do not themselves respond to a *wai* with any physical movement.

If you are staying in Thailand for any length of time, you will gradually learn how to make a *wai*. Watch a company Chairman responding to the *wai* made simultaneously by the members of his Board of Directors with his own collective *wai* while holding a bundle of papers in his right hand and his briefcase in his left hand, but somehow contriving to bring one hand close to the other without dropping anything. See how schoolgirls *wai* and at the same time bob in a curtsy to their teachers, how peasants raise their hands up to their foreheads when greeting a member of the Royal Family, how prominent personalities when seated hold their hands in a mid-way *wai* position of quiet contemplation and reverence while listening to a Buddhist recitation.

Top Tip: Golden Rule for Newcomers

The golden rule for newcomers is to smile at all times, *wai* only when you are quite sure it is the right thing to do and watch closely how the Thais themselves play out this age-old ritual.

The most serious mistake you can make is to wave your hands around in a *wai* to all and sundry, in the mistaken belief that because you have seen something similar in India, it is alright to do the same in Thailand. Thais will be too polite and too shy to correct you; but they will laugh at you, from embarrassment, and you will make a further mistake if you interpret their laughter as pleasure and delight.

THE THAI SMILE

Thailand is indeed known as the Land of Smiles. In the West, we smile because we have something to smile about. In Thailand, people smile naturally, out of sheer *joie de vivre* but also because they have been brought up from an early age to please. To some extent the Thai smile is designed to placate unknown and possibly hostile forces, particularly awkward, red-faced foreigners. So there is something defensive about the Thai smile, designed to put you at ease. Thais do smile, of course, and often laugh at jokes and comic situations, as we do in the West, but harmless personal misfortunes (like being splashed by a passing car or losing a coin down a drain) at which Westerners might chuckle in private, Thais will observe with an open smile on their faces. The intention is not to laugh at you, but to help you psychologically out of your misfortune by sharing your experience and suggesting subliminally that there could be worse calamities!

From this you will gather that Thais are inclined to smile when they are embarrassed. The car behind bumps into you. You get out to remonstrate. The Thai driver is smiling. You resist the temptation to punch him on the nose. Instead, you smile back. His smile is the Thai way of saying sorry. Your smile is your acceptance of his excuses. He will smile back again to say thank you. Three smiles with three different meanings. So tempers are kept on both sides.

Some visitors conclude from all this that Thais are adept at smiling their way out of almost any situation. I suppose, in some ways, this could be true. But after all, why not? Of course, if the driver behind you is driving a truck and demolishes half your car, he is likely to conclude that no amount of smiling will cool your anger; so the chances are that he will simply take to his heels, both to avoid the police and an unpleasant confrontation with you.

Finally, you will notice that nearly all Thai girls smile at you. This is not a 'come hither' appeal (in most cases). It is their way of looking prettier. After all, you would surely prefer smiles to scowls, laughter to grumpy frowns.

BODY MOVEMENTS

Thais are naturally graceful and seem in perfect control of their bodies. Westerners look clumsy, ungainly, uncontrolled and even uncultured. But then Thais are taught from an early age to control their physical movements whereas the emphasis in the West tends to be on free physical expression. Thai girls are taught the elements of traditional dancing, where the main elements are poise, decorum and restraint.

Perhaps the first thing you will notice about social interreaction in Thailand is what the Westerner calls 'high posture/low posture' relations. Traditionally, Thais show respect for elders and superiors by ensuring that they do not loom physically over those higher up the social ladder. So there is a lot of ducking of heads and apparent cringing, which is not cringing at all but solely a display of respect. It used to be standard practice to crawl in the presence of members of the Royal Family. These traditions remain in Thailand today and at all formal occasions Thais will ensure that their heads are below the level of the member of the Royal Family to whom they are speaking.

You make the greatest mistake if you interpret this formalized subservience as out of keeping with Thailand's blossoming democracy. Thais are much attached to their cultural rituals and suggestions from foreigners that such behaviour is 'undemocratic' will be dismissed out of hand.

What you do with your head, hands and feet is, therefore, very important. The head (and hair) being the highest part of your body, are almost sacred. This is why a barber will give you a *wai* before cutting your hair.

Top Tip: Do Not Point Your Feet!

The feet, being the lowest part of your body, are profane. Pointing your feet at someone, particularly at his head, is regarded as insolent behaviour. It can be hard to avoid. Crossing your legs while sitting can lead to one foot unintentionally pointing straight at the head of someone sitting on the other side of the room.

So when seated, try to remember not to cross your legs; worse still is to rest them on another chair or put them on top of your desk.

You should also not step over any part of a person's body, including legs and feet. This may be difficult in a crowded airport waiting-room, but it will show your good manners.

As for your hands, try to keep them under control. Resist the temptation to pat youngsters on the back. Pointing with your fingers is not quite as bad as pointing with your feet, but control your natural (Western) inclination to do so. Beckoning with your hand for someone to come over to you is acceptable, but in Thailand it is done with the palm facing *downwards* as opposed to upwards in the West.

Men should never touch women in public. Of course, times are changing and where youngsters congregate, for instance in Siam Square near Chulalongkorn University in Bangkok, you may see daring youngsters of the opposite sex holding hands. You will, alas, also see foreigners (often overweight, balding, late middle-aged Westerners) holding hands with bar-girls; but that makes well brought-up Thai girls even more circumspect when going out with Western men.

Although the head is considered the most sacred part of the body, the heart (*jai*) is the centre of emotions and intellect. In English we say 'make or change our minds', but in Thai this would be 'make or change our hearts' (*dut sin* or *blien jai*). There are, in fact, so many phrases in Thai using the word '*jai*' that a book has been written trying to explain their meaning in English.

Things are never thrown in Thailand. They are always handed over, preferably with the right hand, and to show respect, with both hands, especially to monks and older people. It is some-times amusing to see a Thai walk four or five yards just to hand you a pencil or eraser. This character-istic may be the reason why Thais are not very good at games such as cricket and baseball;

because of lack of practice, they have difficulty in catching things. On formal occasions, a small gold-coloured round tray with pedestal (*pharn*) is used. If you are presented with something on a *pharn*, just take the item only.

KEEPING YOUR TEMPER

Buddhism is the Middle Path, the avoidance of extremes and violence, the attainment of harmony, inner and external. So Thai behaviour eschews displays of conflict and temper. Keeping a cool heart (*jai yen*) in all possible circumstances is not only ideal behaviour but the norm. Though angry and frustrated, Thais rarely give vent to their feelings. A hot head (*jai rawn* or hot heart) is a social lapse. Westerners are almost expected by Thais to lose their tempers at some point. Placating Thai smiles, alas, sometimes has the opposite effect. The maintenance of superficial harmony, however black your thoughts, may produce under-lying psychological tensions which, when they do come to the surface, lead to violence. The Thai murder rate puts Thailand well up the international league. Avoiding conflict necessarily leads to some superficiality in contacts. Anger in any case might upset malevolent spirits.

Some Thais seem to get drunk easily, possibly because of their light body weight; but in such circumstances friends and even bystanders will try to placate the drunk or smile embarrassingly to excuse his behaviour. A drunken man is, after all, out of control. With a 'hot heart' he may (or malevolent spirits may induce him to) get up to all sorts of mischief, like tossing a hand-grenade at his rival in love, perhaps at a crowded fair-ground.

Like physical violence, verbal violence is equally unbecoming. Criticism is regarded as a form of verbal abuse. Irony and sarcasm are taboo. A dressing-down, even in private, induces resentment. If behaviour is less than ideal, the vaguest of suggestions in due course about how matters might be improved is as far as most Thais would go. An employee dismissed for very good reason may harbour a grudge which could last for years and then suddenly lead to an explosion. A servant summarily dismissed for theft could harbour a long-standing resentment. As a visitor, you are unlikely to find yourself in such situations. But beware of shaking off tourist and night-club touts too physically; their friends may jump on you if you react too strongly to their propositions. At all times, a smile means you know the name of the game.

FACE

Much of what you have read in this chapter is about 'losing face'. Almost anywhere in the East, 'face' is important. There is probably no need to go into further detail here, except to say that Thais will go to great pains to ensure that, so far as possible, you do not lose face. It is almost as though saving the face of others is more important than the risk of losing your own.

4

Festivals, Weddings & Funerals

Festival of Loy Krathong

Thailand has many festivals throughout the year, but the two most popular are Songkhran and Loy Krathong, which are celebrated throughout the country.

SONGKHRAN

Traditionally, this festival celebrates the Thai New Year. It falls on 13 April and lasts for three days. Household Buddha images are cleaned and family members get together to pay their respects to family elders. This is done by presenting them with some small gifts, usually towels or a piece of cloth, and pouring scented water over their hands. Consequently, there is a mass exodus from Bangkok by people returning to their homes in the provinces, and all road, rail and air transportation is fully booked. If you have to go to the airport on 13 April, make sure you allow plenty of time. The highway to the airport is also the main highway to the north and northeast and mammoth traffic jams are inevitable, and the forty-minute trip may take three or four hours!

Since Songkhran occurs in the hottest month of the year, it has become a tradition to throw water over complete strangers. Pretty Thai girls or Westerners dressed in T-shirts are usually the main targets and everything is done in the spirit of fun or *sanuk*. Whereas, formerly, water was thrown from small bowls, high-powered water pistols and buckets are now used. Be prepared for a drenching if you venture out into the streets during this time, especially in the Banglampoo area.

Incidentally, 1 January, the Western New Year, is also celebrated in Thailand in much the same way as in other countries. It has become a tradition to send New Year cards and to present respected elders (family or business) with baskets of fruit or hampers of groceries. These can be obtained at all department stores prior to the New Year and vary in price depending on the contents (which may include XO Brandy and other luxury imported goods). Banks and businesses give away promotional items, such as calendars and diaries, to their clients. Servants are also given a monetary bonus.

LOY KRATHONG

In former days, rivers and canals played a highly significant role in the daily life of the Thai people. They were the source of water for domestic and agricultural use and produced fish for the table, as well as providing an essential method of transportation and a convenient way of waste disposal. The *Loy Krathong* festival is the Thai people's way of thanking and asking forgiveness from *Mae Kongkha*, the Mother of Waters.

Loy Krathong takes place on a full-moon night in October or November, when the water in the rivers is at its highest level. '*Loy*' means to float, and '*krathong*' is a small cup usually made of banana leaves. (Styrofoam *krathongs* are frowned upon because of environmental considerations.) An incense stick, a candle, a coin and flowers are placed in the *krathong* which is then floated down the river. The sight of hundreds of *krathongs*, with their flickering candles, floating down the river under a full moon is truly magical.

WEDDINGS

There is no religious ceremony for weddings in Thailand comparable to the church wedding in

Pouring scented water over bride and groom at a Thai wedding

the West. Although food may be offered to monks in the morning, the Thai wedding is almost a totally secular affair, and can be divided into three distinct activities.

The couple are legally married when they register their marriage at the local district office; if the families are important enough, then the Registration Officer may be invited to the house to register the marriage. The second activity is blessing the bridal couple, and this is what is usually demonstrated at Thai cultural shows performed for tourists.

The bride and groom, dressed in traditional Thai costumes, kneel side by side in a semi-erect position, with their heads slightly bowed and their hands held in front of them in a *wai* position. Their heads are joined together by a thick white cotton thread, called a 'mongkol', symbolizing their union. Guests then take turns in pouring scented water over the hands of the bride and groom. This is usually done with a decorated conch shell, but sometimes a small silver bowl is used.

These two activities, the registration and pouring of scented water, can take place at any time of the day, depending on the most auspicious time worked out by astrologers, and are usually attended by close friends and relatives. However, the third activity, the reception, is invariably held in the evening and attended by all friends and acquaintances of the families concerned.

It is to the reception that you will probably be invited. This usually takes place at about 6.00 pm in the ballroom of a major hotel. In front of the reception hall you will find a long table where you present your gift, which could be money put into the envelope in which you were sent your invitation (this is an easy way of identifying yourself), or any other traditional wedding gift, such as a photo album. Then you sign the reception book and receive a memento of the wedding. The bride and groom, with their parents, stand in line ready to greet you as you enter the reception room.

Weddings are a great place to meet friends and business contacts, and it is quite proper to wander around. When all the guests have arrived, representatives of the bride and groom will make speeches and wish them a long life of wedded bliss; then the bride and groom thank the guests for coming, and this is usually the sign that you can leave. At the door you will again find the bride and groom and their parents ready to bid you farewell.

FUNERALS

As most Thais are Buddhists, they are cremated and most of the rites associated with death are based on Buddhist beliefs. Like weddings, these rites can be divided into three distinct activities: Washing Rites, Funeral Prayers and Cremation. All three normally take place at the *wat* or temple, but in exceptional circumstances, the first may be conducted at the deceased's home. You will probably be invited to the Funeral Prayers and Cremation. Dark suit, white shirt and black tie are considered proper.

Washing Rites

After a person dies, the body is laid on a low table, usually with the face uncovered, with the right hand extended over a large bowl. Close friends and family then take it in turn to pour scented water over the hand into the bowl.

Funeral Prayers

After the Washing Rites, the body is placed in an urn or coffin, depending on the Royal decorations he or she has received, and moved to a *sala* (pavilion). Funeral prayers start at about

7.30 pm and are usually conducted over seven days. Unless you are closely linked to the deceased, it is necessary to attend only once. After arriving at the sala, you light <u>one</u> incense stick and place it in front of the coffin. Then you take your place with the other mourners. A chapter of four monks chant four sets of prayers with short breaks in between. After the third set, refreshments may be served to the mourners. When the prayers are finished, robes and offerings are presented to the monks. Guests can leave any time after the monks have left.

Cremation

The actual cremation may not take place until some time after the person's death. At the *main* (crematorium), guests are handed a small bouquet called *dok mai chan*. Three or four senior guests are then called forward to individually present robes to monks. At the appropriate time, a bell is rung and all guests proceed to the *main* where they place the *dok mai chan* under the coffin. On leaving the *main*, they are usually presented with a small gift to thank them for their attendance.

5

Food, Markets & Eating Out

'. . .the sheer variety [of food] which appeals to foreigners'

Thais love eating; indeed, they seem to spend most of their waking hours nibbling at anything they fancy. With 60 million potential customers, restaurants of all shapes and sizes spring up, if needs be, overnight. Itinerant vendors, sometimes pushing a ramshackle cart or even carrying a food kitchen balanced on a bamboo pole, are everywhere.

If a new building-site opens up, within 24 hours a lean-to shack restaurant will appear, as if by magic, selling noodles, curry and banana fritters. If the food is good, you will see quite respectable people sitting down for their midday meal at very modest pavement kitchens – just a few wooden stools and a couple of rickety, plastic-covered tables.

Thai food has developed remarkably over the last 20 years. It was always there, of course, but it is the sheer variety which appeals to foreigners. So many rice dishes, as well as fish and seafood in so many variations; soups which are a meal in themselves. The variety of Thai food no doubt stems from the fact that Thailand has been a crossroads of the East, with the cuisines of India, China and Malay-Indonesia making their own particular contributions.

Eating in Thailand can be divided into three major categories: snacks, single-dish meals and multi-dish meals. These in turn can be sub-divided into noodles, rice dishes, Thai, Chinese, Indian, etc.

TYPES OF FOOD

Snacks

If someone were to ask me what is the favourite Thai pastime, I would have no hesitation in replying 'eating', and this is manifested in the hundreds of snacks, mostly sold by street vendors, that are available everywhere and range from chicken on skewers to fresh guava, pineapple, watermelon, grilled and fried bananas, etc. Try them, and you will be surprised at the difference between what you can buy in the West and the 'real thing'.

Single-Dish Meals

These are usually eaten for lunch by the local people and are equivalent to the 'fast foods' of the West. There are two main categories – rice dishes and noodles. Rice (*kao*) dishes consist of a plate of rice with a topping, such as chicken with basil, various curries, red or crispy pork and duck. Noodles (*guey-tiel*) come dry (*haeng*) or in broth (*nam*). There are four main types: large (*sen yai*), small (*sen lek*), tiny (*sen mee*) and egg (*sen bamee*). Won ton is known as *giew* in Thailand.

There are so many combinations of rice and noodle dishes that it would be impossible to list them all. One way to try them is at 'Food Centres' located in all major shopping centres. Here there is a common dining area with 20 or 30 booths selling different single-dish meals. The plates and cutlery are supplied by the shopping centre and you have to buy coupons (usually about 100 bahts worth and are valid only on the day of purchase) at strategically located counters. You can then wander round and select whatever takes your fancy. Unused coupons can be refunded for cash, but only on the same day. A good example of this type of Food Centre is located on the top floor of the Mah Boon Krong Shopping Centre.

Multi-Dish Meals

This is the way that Thais eat at home or in restaurants. Each person is given a plate of rice and there are three or four communal dishes of vegetable, pork, beef and fish which are placed at the centre of the table. Each person takes what he wants, usually from one dish at a time, and eats it with his rice. This is very practical as you take only what appeals to you, and may have given rise to the famous 'Eastern hospitality', because if an unexpected visitor arrives, all you have to do is add an extra plate of rice and he can join the meal. In the West, if you have four pork chops for four people and someone arrives unexpectedly, what do you do?

In Chinese restaurants, guests usually sit at a round table with a revolving top. Food is served in courses and each course is eaten in turn. At more formal dinners, a waiter will serve each guest, but normally, guests serve themselves. Sometimes you may find your neighbour serving you, but this is quite normal and you should return the compliment. There are usually about eight or nine courses, and in Thailand, you know you have come to the last course when fried rice is served.

An increasingly popular type of meal is the Buffet Lunch or Dinner. These are usually provided by hotels and the advantage is that a large variety of dishes are available – Thai, Japanese and Western. For instance, the lunch buffet at the Siam City Hotel has a number of Thai dishes, a roast, salads, cold cuts, sashimi, sushi, fresh oysters, smoked salmon, etc., all for about 350 Baht ++ (the ++ after a price means plus service charge and plus government tax).

At restaurants serving Thai food, a fork and spoon are the only eating utensils. Chopsticks are generally used for noodles and at Chinese restaurants. Knives are rarely used when eating non-Western food. The fork and spoon you use will, incidentally, last you throughout the meal, whether the dishes change from spicy ('hot') to sweet and sour, salty or pungent. Dishes may be served piping hot, but are eaten even when cold. Make sure you know which sauce goes with which dish as sauces (or 'nam jim') can make all the difference to a meal.

Thais appreciate good food, but they do not belch or lick their fingers in public. You should begin eating as soon as the food is put in front of you. Conversation is considered proper during meals.

Top Tip: The Insider's Guide to Spicy Food

Some Thai food can be very spicy; peppers can be bad enough, but some chillies will take the roof off your mouth and bring tears to your eyes. If this happens to you, take some water and counteract the spice with plain rice or some sweet dish, even a spoonful of sugar. If you are drinking beer with your meal do not attempt to 'cool down' by drinking more of it: instead you should not touch a drop for at least five minutes!

WHO PAYS?

If a Thai invites you to a restaurant, he will naturally expect to pay. You will notice that he does not leave a tip, except perhaps a few baht for the waitress. This is because a service charge is invariably included or assumed to be included and, in any case, tipping is not a widespread custom. If you go on a business trip to Thailand, it could be that you should pay if you are the most senior person present.

Guessing the status of other people is one of the more sensitive social preoccupations of Thais and so much depends on your assessment of the age, family connections and wealth of others present, and their assessment of you. Potentially, much 'face' is at stake, particularly if you or your colleagues get it wrong. As a person of status, you are expected to do the honours and your failure to do so, or to offer only to split the bill, will not only make you lose status in the eyes of your Thai hosts, but may cause offence as well. If you wish to retain respect, be prepared to pay as required.

From all this, you may perhaps have concluded that status and respect may be bought in Thailand. Sadly, this is true in many cases, and the desire to acquire money, and thereby status, has undermined many traditional values. Hence the rise in sex-related activities, such as prostitution, massage parlours and bars, where money can be obtained quickly and easily. In a society where prostitution is endemic, many young women aspire to money because money brings power and power brings status. Money is the means to social redemption; the loss of face in prostitution may be more than compensated for by the acquisition of the means to improve one's status eventually.

SOME WELL-KNOWN MARKETS

In reality, the whole of Bangkok is one vast market and a shopper's paradise. Formerly, farmers and other people from upcountry used to bring their products to sell in the cities, but since the manufacturing boom in Thailand a few years ago, young entrepreneurs have taken over city sidewalks to sell every conceivable type of goods, from designer clothes to electronic equipment, and this has caused many problems, because on many streets pedestrians have nowhere to walk and vendors have spilled over onto the road surface, adding even more confusion to the already chaotic traffic. There are however a number of traditional markets which should be visited since each has a unique character of its own.

Chatuchak Weekend Market

Open 6.00 am to sunset, Saturdays and Sundays. With nearly 8,000 stalls and covering an area of about 28,000 square metres, this is the biggest market in Thailand. The organizers have tried grouping the same type of stalls together, but this has proved to be an impossible task. Your best bet is just to wander and try to take in everything. Some of the more interesting are handicrafts from all parts of Thailand, ceramics, antiques, tropical fish, birds (including fighting cocks), plants, stamps and coins, collectibles, books, paintings, . . . the list goes on and on. If you have time, cross the road and visit the Farmers' Organization Market. Here you will find an enormous selection of local fruits and vegetables, fresh seafood, and huge pots of ready-to-eat meals (the Thai version of 'Take-Home'/'To Go'). Chatuchak Weekend Market is situated near the Northern Bus Terminal. Because of the popularity of this market, there are plans to keep it open all week.

Pak Klong Dalat

This is the wholesale Bangkok Flower Market where large bundles of orchids and other exotic tropical flowers can be seen. There are also shops that specialize in making funeral wreaths and bouquets. The market is near the Chao Phraya River at the foot of the Memorial Bridge (*Saphan Phut*).

Klong Thom Market

Sometimes known as the Thieves' Market, Klong Thom is famous for calculators, watches, toys and some goods of dubious origin. Recently, the city authorities have relocated many of the vendors to other locations in order to ease traffic congestion. A visit to Klong Thom market can easily be combined with a visit to Bangkok's Chinatown which is right next door.

Banglampoo Market

This market is well-known for its vast array of clothing. Most Bangkok office girls shop here, but more casual wear, such as jeans and T-shirts, is also available. It is located near Tanao Road where many of the cheap guest houses for back-packers are located. There are also one or two second-hand bookstalls on Tanao Road selling English, French and German books.

Market aficionados should be warned that street vending in Bangkok is banned on Wednesdays to allow pavements to be hosed down.

As a result of the economic crisis which began in the second half of 1997, many 'boot-markets' have sprung up, especially at the weekends. A parking area is set aside where people can, for a small fee, sell any unwanted personal articles they may have. These are great fun, and although goods consist mainly of clothing, shoes, bric-a-brac, etc., you can sometimes come across real finds. The most famous of these markets is the 'Market of the Formerly Rich' on Soi Thonglor, held on Saturdays and Sundays, where light aircraft and diamond-studded Rolex watches can be found.

6

Business &
Entertainment

Decorated parasols from Chiang Mai

BUSINESS CULTURE

The rules about social behaviour and entertaining apply very much to business relations as well. Because Bangkok is such a sprawling metropolis and the traffic at times so exasperating that it can take you well over an hour to get across town, you will probably find that you can, with luck, make only two business calls in the morning and only one in the afternoon. This tends not to leave all that much time for entertaining your business contacts, even if you and they would like to get together.

Business lunches are very acceptable and the better-class restaurants provide a crisp, but relaxed service. As many Bangkok businessmen leave home at 6.00 or 6.30 in the morning, they are usually ready for lunch at 12.00. Many people, especially government officials, leave for lunch at 11.30. Thais on the whole prefer Thai or Chinese food, but will gladly eat Western food if the opportunity occurs. (For some reason, lamb and mutton have a very strong smell for Thais, and they usually cannot eat it unless it is smothered in spices.)

As mentioned earlier, nearly all hotels have buffet lunches and these are popular as they cater for all tastes. Nouvelle cuisine is still very much in vogue at the top-class restaurants like the Normandie Grill in the Oriental Hotel and Le Cristal at the Regent. Low calorie, salad-oriented business lunches for the health-conscious businessman are catching on only slowly.

Inviting your business contacts out to an evening meal needs careful judgement. On the whole, Thais like to get away from the office by 4.30 or 5.00 pm at the latest and are frankly not all that interested in hanging around in town until dinner time, which can be as early as 6.30 pm. If your associates are sufficiently senior and Westernized, they will understand the importance of relaxed entertainment when those controversial clauses in the deal under negotiation can perhaps be finally agreed.

Top Tip: Choose Informal Entertainment

Although they may be too polite to say so, a formal dinner is likely to be, for most except Board-level representatives, something of an ordeal. If you can contrive more informal entertainment in very casual attire (buffet dinner on a river launch, a private room in a popular restaurant), this is likely to find far greater favour with your Thai guests.

Everyone in Thailand has a business card, even the management trainees. There is no need to bring a great quantity with you as you can have them printed very easily in Thailand. Simple cards with no company logo can be printed in half an hour at any major shopping centre. More complicated cards will need a professional printer but the service is very fast, efficient and inexpensive. Insist on examining the proofs and do so very carefully as mistakes can be time-consuming and hard to rectify.

Some years ago it used to be fashionable to have your cards printed in Thailand in English on one side and in Thai on the other, but this practice is waning as knowledge of English increases and, frankly, is no longer either necessary or desirable. Most Thais (and even some

Westerners!) acknowledge that spelling in any language is only a rough guide to pronunciation, so that your English-language visiting card is adequate in itself. But do try and include as much detail as possible, including your telephone, telex, fax, e-mail and even home number. It helps to build up your status and personality.

EASTERN MYSTERIES

Finally, a word of advice about those special payments which some say are essential to doing business out East. Find yourself a reliable local agent and listen to his advice. Should he feel that for any reason it might be prudent to offer a commission, technical fee, research charge, agency split or any other euphemistic payment, let him attend to this in his own way. Above all, do not let yourself get involved in passing money in brown paper envelopes under the table to individuals who have somehow convinced you that the secret of success lies in their personal remuneration on the side. You will invariably pass the wrong sort of money, at the wrong time, to the wrong people.

Instead, take the perfectly respectable view that, as a Westerner, you cannot possibly begin to understand these mysteries. All local firms have local fixers. Never forget that, for public sector contracts, there is a formidable Counter Corruption Commission which can (and does) descend on unwary public servants and take them and their books away for minute investigation. You should also know that some of the most successful Western firms in Bangkok have never ever resorted to illegal payments, precisely because there are so many legal ways in which these delicate matters can be satisfactorily resolved, to everyone's mutual satisfaction.

A NIGHT OUT ON THE TOWN

Thais can be very hospitable, even lavish with their entertainment; it enhances their status and they regard money spent on having fun (*sanuk*) as money well spent. They will not expect you to reciprocate in Thailand, nor to 'stand the next round'.

Bangkok's night life is world-famous. Provided you watch your spending, a night out on the town can be relatively inexpensive. There are a thousand-and-one distractions for males. For couples, the flashy discos and more intimate videotheques, the jazz and dixie-land night spots, even the go-go bars can be a lot of fun. Women are welcomed, and safe, almost anywhere, but are unlikely to want to stay for the duration. As a single woman, it is best to go in company; two women can enjoy the scene, but not much else.

Most males make their way to Patpong, three street blocks in an area between Silom and Suriwongse Roads. Patpong 1 and 2 cater principally for Western and English-speaking tourists, Patpong 3 for Japanese. There are a range of ground-floor bars, with gyrating go-go girls, the music not quite as ear-splitting as in the discos. The bar-girls will chat you up, but not pester you. Their English is limited. You can stay for about half an hour on one beer (Baht 60) and a coke (Baht 50) or two for the girl who sits with you. [Note: The current rate is Baht 50 = $1]. You can then move on to another ground-floor bar, or venture upstairs to one of the first-floor establishments which have even more scantily-dressed girls and will offer floor shows as well. Prices are double, if not treble, the ground-floor establishments and what you see, particularly during the floor shows, may make your eyes pop, so I suggest that you do not go upstairs if you are easily shocked.

Apart from Patpong, there are similar complexes at Soi ('lane') Cowboy and at the Nana Entertainment complex. You might also try a massage, either traditional style (perfectly respectable) or at one of the tourist massage parlours (where anything goes). The larger massage parlours along Petchaburi Road nowadays mostly cater for locals and some masseuses are reluctant to take on Westerners because of growing concern about AIDS.

The bar-girls and masseuses who service the tourist industry have become something of a legend. By and large, they are not the kind of toughened hustlers who operate in West European countries. Most of them come to Bangkok hoping to make about Baht 100,000 over five years, enough for them to return home up-country and open a dress-making shop or beauty salon, and hopefully to settle down and marry (a second time: their first marriage is generally disastrous, which may be why they came to Bangkok in the first place). They will laugh and cry with you, but some of them are not as sophisticated as they seem and are learning about AIDS the hard way.

Dotted around Bangkok are what are described as 'Member Clubs'. These are for local businessmen, not for foreign tourists. As a casual visitor, you will pay through the nose, so do not venture inside unless you are taken by a Thai friend at his expense.

Top Tip: Dealing with Hustlers

One final word of advice: if ever you find yourself being hustled by a bar owner, do not react violently, but as soon as you get outside, ask for help from the ever-watchful Tourist Police and, without too much trouble, you will get your money back.

Traditional Thai architecture

7

Travelling in Thailand

Tuk-tuks

As a visitor to Thailand, you may wish to do some travelling on your own. The main domestic airline, Thai Airways, now amalgamated with Thai International, has frequent services to all major destinations in Thailand (Boeing 737s and Airbus). In Bangkok, the domestic terminal is next to the international terminal and a free shuttle service is provided. Another domestic airline, Bangkok Airways, flies to a number of destinations, of which the most popular is Koh Samui, the resort island in the Gulf of Thailand. There is also a good railway network and buses and coaches of all description. Be careful when travelling during major holidays, such as Songkhran and the New Year, as all means of transportation are fully booked.

TAXIS AND TUK-TUKS

Nearly all taxis in Bangkok now have meters, although some drivers are reluctant to use them. Initial fare is 35 Baht. No tip is expected, but the passenger has to pay any expressway fees. Most major hotels have a limousine service which can be hired for the day or for a specific destination; naturally, they are much more expensive than taxis.

'Tuk-tuks', or motorized three-wheel scooters, are popular with backpackers but they do not provide much protection from the elements or the pollution of Bangkok. Fares must be agreed upon before starting the journey, so do not get into the tuk-tuk before this is done. Many tuk-tuk drivers are young men from the Northeast and cannot resist the lure of an open road, so some journeys can be hair-raising.

As most taxi and tuk-tuk drivers know very little English, the major problem is making your destination known. The easiest way of overcoming this is to ask a Thai to write down the destination for you. Never hail a taxi or tuk-tuk with your foot.

Motorcycle taxis are a relatively new method of transportation which has evolved as a result of the traffic situation in Bangkok. Formerly, they were used to take passengers from the main road to their destinations in the small lanes that are not serviced by buses. However, when the traffic is at a standstill, which is quite often, they may be the only means available of reaching your destination in time. Helmets are compulsory on the main roads, but motorcycle taxis always have a spare one for their passengers. As sitting on the back of a motorcycle weaving through dense traffic can be heart-stopping, this method of transportation should only be used in dire emergencies.

BUSES AND BOATS

There are four types of buses in Bangkok: executive, air-conditioned, ordinary and green. Executive buses are limited to about 20 seats (no standing) and have air-conditioning, TV, newspapers and telephones. There is a flat rate of 40 Baht per trip irrespective of distance. Unfortunately, there are not too many routes but more are being planned. Air-conditioned buses have more routes but tend to be more crowded. Fares start at 6 Baht and depend on the length of the journey. Ordinary buses are the principal means of transportation in Bangkok and consequently can become very crowded, especially during the morning and evening rush-hours. Fares are 3.5 Baht per trip. Green buses are privately owned and have a concession to supplement ordinary buses. Fares are 3.50 Baht per trip. Maps with bus routes can be purchased at bookstores.

AIRPORT BUS SERVICE

A new Airport Bus Service to and from Don Muang Airport (for both international and domestic terminals) has recently been introduced. There are three routes, as follows:

A1:   Silom Road, serving the business area

A2:   Sanam Luang, serving the older part of town and stopping at Banglampoo, the area where cheap guest houses and hostels for backpackers are located

A3:   Thonglor, serving the residential area along Sukhumvit Road and stopping at the Eastern Bus Terminal (for buses to Pattaya)

The fare is 70 Baht per person and there is space for luggage. The service is fast and efficient, but due to traffic conditions, there may be long delays between buses, so allow plenty of time, especially for the journey to the airport.

A nother way of getting around is by boat and there are frequent services along the Chao Phraya river. Most landings supply you with details of the service. Passenger ferries also cross the river at strategic points and cost one Baht per trip.

Buses also connect Bangkok with nearly every part of the country. Some are very comfortable but it can become very crowded when there are holidays. There are three terminals which serve different regions: Northern Bus Terminal (Mor Chit) for the North and Northeast; Eastern Bus Terminal (Ekkamai) for the East and the Southern Bus Terminal (Pin Klao) for the South.

When travelling on buses, whether in the city or up-country, it is customary to give due respect to monks. Try to give them space; women must never come into physical contact with them.

TRAINS

Trains are another popular way of travelling up-country. However, trains are slower than buses and routes are limited. Overnight sleepers to popular destinations such as Chiang Mai and Haad Yai are well patronized. The same rule concerning monks applies to trains as well as buses.

CARS

Cars may be hired. As in Britain (and Malaysia, Singapore, Indonesia, Hong Kong and Japan), cars drive on the left. The speed limit in towns is 60 kms per hour and 100 kms per hour in the country. After overtaking, you are expected to move back into the left-hand lane; there is generally no 'slow' lane as in Europe, unless it is specifically designated. Most road signs are in Thai, warning signs included. You may feel it better to hire a driver as well, which will only add another 25–30 per cent to the cost of the hire. If you do want to drive yourself, a valid international driving licence is required.

Be warned that up-country heavy trucks will not necessarily get out of your way on narrow roads and bus drivers sometimes drive too fast trying to meet schedules in very difficult conditions. There have been some appalling accidents. If you are involved in a minor accident, as a foreigner you are assumed to be richer and so are expected to pay (your higher status, hence your privilege). In more serious accidents, the other driver is likely to have the advantage of speaking fluent Thai, but he might flee the scene if he has no licence or is blatantly in the wrong.

Top Tip: Be Wary of Hiring Motor Cycles!

Hire cars only from hotels and reliable agencies. Even then, check on insurance. Beware of hiring motor cycles at holiday resorts. They may not be insurable and could be technically defective. Sadly, many young foreigners do themselves serious injury on these contraptions.

Bangkok traffic is becoming more and more aggressive as more cars and more motor-cycles compete for limited road space. Traffic jams in Bangkok are notorious and you can be stuck in one place for two or three hours. Although both short- and long-term remedial action, such bus-lanes, one-way roads, expressways, mass transit systems. etc., are being undertaken it will be some time before the situation improves.

Be warned also that pedestrian crossings (zebra crossings) are not inviolate as in some Western countries. Cars may not stop, so be extra careful when crossing roads. It is always advisable to use overpasses whenever possible. Beware also of motor-cycles and buses coming from an unexpected direction in bus lanes.

CLOTHING

Westerners visiting Thailand will find the climate hot and Bangkok can at times be particularly oppressive and debilitating, so clothing should be light, loose and airy. Thailand has a booming ready-to-wear market, so a lot of good quality inexpensive clothing can be purchased locally. Thais are modest in clothing and most people prefer to cover up against the sun when outside. Foreigners, on the other hand, tend to undress as far as they dare even in town (and at beaches more than they should). Natural fibres, such as cotton, are much to be preferred to synthetics. Most men wear short-sleeved shirts when at leisure, but long sleeves are sometimes worn in better-class restaurants, where the air-conditioning can be fierce. You will rarely see Thai women with bare shoulders, and flimsy dresses in air-conditioned establishments can ruin an evening.

It is not too difficult to spot the less culturally-conscious visitor to Thailand. He could well be wearing shorts which reveal hairy legs while his chest is covered by an undersize T-shirt. His huge physical frame (occasionally with a beer belly) makes him appear slightly grotesque to Thais. She might be wearing a mini-skirt or shorts and something skimpy above. This lack of modesty is regarded by Thais as thoroughly bad taste. But tourism is an important money-spinner (some seven million tourists – mostly from Asia – now bring in around US$8.6 billion annually), so allowances are made; in any case, as a foreigner, you are likely to find yourself paying rather more in entrance fees to various establishments than the locals, an issue which gives rise to perpetual controversy in the local English-language press.

Westerners who live in Thailand for any length of time soon adapt to the sartorial customs of the country; lightweight trousers (pants) for men, sports shirts and fairly sturdy sandals. At the beaches, topless bathing is just possible in some areas (parts of Phuket and offshore islands like Ko Amui and Ko Samet), but most Thais regard it as silly; who wants to get sun-burnt and invite skin cancer? Thai girls go to great lengths to keep the sun off their skin; the paler their skin, the greater their imagined beauty.

VISITING TEMPLES

As noted earlier, one of the most attractive features of Thai culture are the Buddhist temples to be found all over the country, even in smaller villages. In Bangkok and other towns, the temples (*wat*) can be very elaborate, ornate constructions. The most important building in a *wat* is the *bot*; this is where the main Buddha image is housed and where important ceremonies, such as ordinations, are performed.

Monks usually practise meditation, hold meetings and preach sermons in *viharn*. The *kuti*, or monks' living quarters, are off-limits to women. Other buildings may house Buddha images donated to the *wat* over the years. These images do not represent the Buddha as a deity, but are meant to help the individual through contemplation of the image's serenity, in his progress towards enlightenment. Nevertheless, all Buddha images, no matter the size, should be treated with the utmost respect.

While Thais are tolerant for the most part when foreigners 'put their foot in it,' they are likely to be seriously upset by unseemly tourist behaviour in temples; wearing a T-shirt and shorts when visiting a *wat* could be thought very bad taste and you might be asked to leave. Pay attention to any restrictions on photographing within the *bot*.

As mentioned earlier, women are not allowed in the monks' living quarters; nor may they hand anything directly to a monk. If an occasion arises, at a religious ceremony for example, where a woman has to present something to a monk, the monk will spread a piece of cloth in front of him and the object should be placed on this. Women may, however, speak directly to monks who, in Bangkok at least, are only too keen to practise their English. Women should never touch a monk or his robes.

'Visitors to temples should remove their shoes. . .'

68

8

The Thai Language

ก	ไก่	ก เอ๋ย ก ไก่
ข	ไข่	วางขาย
ค	ควาย	ใช้งาน
ฆ	ระฆัง	ข้างฝา
ง	งู	เลื้อยคลาน

First five letters of the Thai alphabet set out as a children's rhyme to assist learning

The Thais mostly came from China and, not surprisingly, their language is related to Chinese. There are many Thai-speaking peoples (known by the generic description 'Tai') living outside the borders of Thailand including, for example, Laos, Vietnam, Yunnan in southern China, Burma, and as far afield as Assam in northern India.

ALPHABET

Thai is written from left to right in one continuous stream, without gaps between words and with virtually no punctuation or capital letters. The alphabet is of fairly distant Indian origin and is akin to the Burmese, Lao and Khmer alphabets. There are 44 consonants (but only 28 consonantal sounds), 24 vowels and diphthongs and 4 tone marks (meaning different things for different classes of consonant).

Westerners find it takes a long time to learn to speak or write Thai, and even many of those who have lived most of their lives in Thailand can still only just get by in the spoken language. If it is any consolation, Thais find their own language not that easy to master.

SPOKEN LANGUAGE

The spoken language is mainly a problem for Westerners because of the tones. A simple word may mean several things depending on how it is pronounced:

sua (rising) [pronounced like 'sewer'] means a tiger
sua (falling) means a shirt
sua (low tone) means a mat

Here are some of the meanings of the sound *'chai'*, with various spellings and tones:

fringe	to pass near	to send
end	to use	to pierce
to blow lightly	man	to spend

to glance	to be	to need
to blend	yes	victory

The tone is as important as the spelling of the word. Both must be learnt together. Westerners tend to make the mistake of learning the word first and hoping they will remember the tone later. Thai children learn both word and tone simultaneously. Better to do it their way.

All consonants at the end of syllables are simplified. When spoken, however they may be spelt, they end only in the hard sounds *p, t* and *k* or *m, n, ng, w* and *y*. This is why words ending with an *l* are pronounced with a final *n*. 'Oriental Hotel' becomes naturally 'Orienten Hoten' and 'Central Department Store' becomes 'Centren'. The word for 'bill', now used in Thai is 'bin.' In the spoken language, the *l* and *r* in the non-final position are not interchangeable. It is a sign of an educated person if he can get these consonants correct. The most difficult sound for a foreigner is the initial *ng*, such as *ngarn* (work) or *ngern* (money), as there is no equivalent in Western languages. Remember also that adjectives come after nouns, so that 'red ant' becomes 'ant red', or *mot daeng*.

FORMS OF ADDRESS

Depending on your perceived status and social standing, there are a whole range of personal pronouns in everyday use where in English we use only 'I', 'me' and 'you'. Safe words are *pom* (men only) and *dichan* (women only) for I/me and *khun* for you (men and women). In English, whether you say 'Sir' or 'Ma'am' depends on the sex of the person to whom you are talking. In Thai, it depends on the speaker. A man will always say '*kraap*' and a woman '*kah*' irrespective of the sex of the person spoken to. These two words are used a great deal in Thai since they denote good manners and politeness.

Top Tip: Always Use First Names

Remember to call men and women by their first (given) name. Almost all Thais have a nickname given to them at birth, usually denoting some characteristic such as 'Black' or 'Fat'. Sometimes it is a tradition. I know a family whose nicknames were 'Tiger, Bear, Elephant, Crocodile and Rhinoceros'. These nicknames stay with you all your life and people become very attached to them.

Originally, the only names Thais had were first names; family names were introduced comparatively recently earlier this century, many by a Royal Decree of King Vajiravudh (Rama VI). First names are generally very much shorter than family names which may have complex Pali or Sanskrit spellings, but are modernized in pronunciation. The polite form of address is *Khun* for both men and women. Thus you would address Mr Suthep Chantavimol as 'Khun Suthep' and his wife Mrs Pranom Chantavimol as 'Khun Pranom'. So you can see Thailand has had Women's Lib a long time before the West. Khun is used for both men and women, married and unmarried!

Thais, knowing that foreigners find their language almost impossible to learn, will be delighted if you make the effort to say a few words in their language. Here are a few useful words and phrases:

GENERAL VOCABULARY

khop khun maak	thank you very much
kaw toht	sorry, excuse me
mai dee	bad, not good
dee maak	very good
yai kern bai	too big
lek kern bai	too small
bai cha cha	go slowly
bai rew rew	go quickly
trong bai	straight ahead
liew sai	turn left
liew kwaar	turn right
pood thai mai dai	I cannot speak Thai
. . .yoo thi nai?	Where is. . .?
mai sarp	I don't know (something)
mai ow	I don't want
prung nee	tomorrow
wan nee	today
mua wan nee	yesterday

NUMBERS

neung	one
sawng	two
saam	three
see	four
haa	five
hok	six
jet	seven
baet	eight
gao	nine
sib	ten
sib neung, sib sawng	eleven, twelve, etc.
yee sib	twenty
yee sib neung, yee sib sawng	twenty-one, twenty-two, etc.
saam sib, see sib	thirty, forty, etc.
roi	100
pun	1,000
meun	10,000
saen	100,000
larn	million

IMPORTANT NOTE: Some commercial tourist sites have double pricing, one for Thais and one for foreigners, on the assumption that foreigners are richer. The Thai price will be given in Thai numerals and the foreigners' price in Arabic numerals. Although this practice is frowned upon, it still persists in some areas.

Facts About Thailand

Thailand covers an area of 513,000 sq kms and is about the size of France. It has 2,400 kms of coastline, with the Gulf of Thailand to the East and the Andaman Sea to the West. It is a Constitutional Monarchy with the King as Head of State.

The capital, Bangkok (Krung Thep Mahanakhon in Thai), has a population of around 9 million. Other centres of population are Chiang Mai (North), Nakhon Ratchasima (Northeast) and Haad Yai (South).

Thailand's Seasons

Thailand has only three seasons: cool, hot and rainy. The cool season, from November to February, is probably the best time to visit and temperatures drop to about 25 degrees centigrade. During the hot season, from March to June, temperatures can rise to 40 degrees centigrade. The rainy season brings some relief from the heat, but humidity is much higher. In October, when rain water from the north meets high tides in the Gulf of Thailand, there is considerable flooding in many parts of Bangkok.

The currency is the Baht which is divided into 100 Satang. There are 1,000 Baht, 500 Baht, 100 Baht, 50 Baht, 20 Baht and 10 Baht notes. Coins are issued in 10 Baht, 5 Baht, 1 Baht, 50 Satang and 25 Satang denominations.

Banks are open 9.30 am to 3.30 pm. Cash can be obtained from ATMs by using credit cards or bank cards displaying the Plus or Cirrus symbols. Most credit cards are accepted, with the most popular being Visa and Master Card.

Thailand uses the metric system, and the electricity is 220 volts. Flat American-type plugs are used.

Public telephones are abundant and can be either coin or card operated. International Direct Dialling (IDD) is available in most places. To access, dial 001 + country code + area code + number.

Tourist Police

The Tourist Police is a special unit set up to assist tourists, and members, recognized by their sleeve badges, can usually speak English. They can be contacted at 221-6206 (Bangkok), 248-974 (Chiang Mai) and 212-213 (Phuket).

Currently, there are two English-language newspapers, *The Bangkok Post* and *The Nation*. CNN and BBC are available at most major hotels.

Thailand has no national religion, although 90% of the population is Buddhist (there are over 300 *wats* in Bangkok alone). All religions coexist peacefully, and you may find a Buddhist temple side-by-side with a mosque or a Christian church.

National Holidays

January 1	New Year's Day
Early February	Makha Bucha (religious)
April 6	Chakri Day
April 13-15	Songkhran Festival (Thai New Year)
May 1	Labour Day
May 5	Coronation Day
May 8	Royal Ploughing Ceremony
May 10	Visakha Bucha (religious)
July 8	Asarnha Bucha (religious)
August 12	H.M. The Queen's Birthday
October 23	Chulalongkorn Day
December 5	H.M. The King's Birthday
December 10	Constitution Day
December 31	New Year's Eve

Although tapwater is theoretically safe to drink, to be on the safe side, you should stick to bottled water or soft drinks.

Medical and dental services in Bangkok are excellent. Most private clinics are open at 5.30 pm, after doctors finish their shift in hospitals. All hospitals provide a 24-hour emergency service. Take precautions against malaria when travelling upcountry, especially near the Burmese border.

Word of Warning

A final word of warning: the use, possession and trading of drugs is strictly prohibited. NEVER be persuaded by a 'friend' to take a present back home, and always do your packing yourself. Other prohibited articles are antiques and religious artefacts (the former need written permission from the Fine Arts Department, and the latter from the Religious Affairs Department).

With the installation of a new Bangkok Governor, an Anti-littering Campaign has been launched and there are heavy fines for littering. So be careful when you throw away your cigarette stubs, tissues, plastic bags, etc.

Thai Words Used In This Book

Index